# THE CAMEL

## HIS

## ORGANIZATION HABITS AND USES

# THE CAMEL

## HIS

## ORGANIZATION HABITS AND USES

CONSIDERED WITH

## REFERENCE TO HIS INTRODUCTION INTO THE UNITED STATES

GEORGE P MARSH

GYAN

*Published by*

Gyan Publishing House
5, Ansari Road
Daryaganj, New Delhi-110002
Phone: 011-47034999, 9811692060
E-mail: books@gyanbooks.com

*Distribution Network*
gyanbooks.com
India, USA, Canada, UK, Australia, France



ISBN : 978-81-212-9348-8 (PB)
First Published, 1856

2nd Impression 2023

*Printed at:* Gyan Press, Delhi.



**THE CAMEL HIS ORGANIZATION HABITS AND USES**
Author: GEORGE P MARSH

# THE CAMEL

HIS

# ORGANIZATION HABITS AND USES

CONSIDERED WITH

REFERENCE TO HIS INTRODUCTION INTO THE UNITED STATES

BY

GEORGE P MARSH

BOSTON
GOULD AND LINCOLN
59 WASHINGTON STREET
NEW YORK: SHELDON, BLAKEMAN & CO
CINCINNATI: GEORGE S BLANCHARD
1856

# PREFACE.

THE practicability and expediency of introducing the camel into the United States having long since engaged my attention as a problem of much economical interest, I availed myself of the facilities afforded by a late residence of some years in the Turkish empire, to investigate the subject more fully than it had been in my power to do in this country. Several months of travel in Egypt, Nubia, Arabia Petræa and Syria, presented opportunities for a good deal of personal observation, and I occasionally saw the Turcoman camel, and others of northern breeds, employed at different points in Asia Minor, and sometimes at Constantinople. I also gathered such information as I was able by inquiry and correspondence, and by consulting the books of travel and natural history to which I had access. By these means, I arrived at a strong persuasion of the probable success of a judiciously conducted attempt to naturalize in the new world this oldest of domestic quadrupeds, and at the same time I collected most of the materials which compose the following pages. Since my return to the United States, I have added to my previous sources of information Ritter's valuable and learned essay, Die geographische Verbreitung des Kameels, in the thirteenth volume of his Erdkunde, Carbuccia's work on the Dromedary of Algeria, Hammer-Purgstall's erudite paper, Das Kamel, in the sixth volume of the Denkschriften der Kaiserlichen Akademie der Wissenschaften in Wien, and some other instructive treatises on the same subject. All these I have used freely, generally referring to chapter or page, though I may, very probably, have sometimes neglected to give credit, particularly in stating facts of almost universal notoriety. To save frequent reference, I remark here, once for all, that the passages embraced in quotation marks, without reference to the source, are borrowed from an article entitled "The Desert," in the ninety-first number of the American Whig Review, or from an unpublished journal of eastern travel by the author of that article. I ought also to add, that I have embodied in this volume the contents of a lecture delivered by me at the Smithsonian Institution in the winter of 1854–5, and printed with one of the Reports of that Institution.

The results of my own observations have in general accorded with those of previous inquirers. I have not the vanity to suppose that I have added anything to the existing stock of knowledge respecting an animal which has been an object of enlightened curiosity to naturalists and travellers for more than twenty centuries; and, so far as possible, I have preferred rather to cite the testimony of well-known writers than to seem to claim the merit of discovery, by stating, on my own authority, facts which others had observed before me. Besides this, it has been agreeable to me thus to bear witness to the accuracy of observation and fidelity of description which characterize the writings of Tavernier, and Erman, and Bergmann, and Denham, and Burckhardt, and other votaries and too often victims of science, whose labors have done so much to facilitate the researches of later explorers in the same attractive field of knowledge.

The information which I have thus collected, and which I now lay before the public, has an important bearing on a question that the American government is bringing to a practical test. If the experiment shall fail, it will be neither because the attempt is in its nature hopeless, nor because the public agent entrusted with the charge of it, has committed any error in the execution of his duties, but because the means appropriated by Congress did not admit of an experiment on a scale extensive enough, and varied enough, to embrace all the reasonable chances of success. In any event, the present able Secretary of War, is entitled to no little credit for the intelligence and zeal with which he has urged this interesting and important measure; and it is earnestly to be hoped, that the national legislature will not refuse any further appropriation necessary to give a full and fair trial to a project which promises so valuable results.

I may be thought perhaps to have unnecessarily crowded my volume with details and citations, but I have intended to take a purely practical view of my subject, and I have therefore sought to condense into the limits I have prescribed to myself the greatest possible amount of information, and to fortify my statements by the most reliable authorities. The theme, if not unimportant, is humble, and I claim no merit but that of fidelity in presenting the conclusions at which I have arrived.

THE AUTHOR.

BURLINGTON, Vermont, June 1, 1856.

# CONTENTS.

## CHAPTER IV.



## CHAPTER V.



## CHAPTER VI.



## CHAPTER VII.



## CHAPTER VIII.



## CHAPTER IX.

## CHAPTER X.



## CHAPTER XI.



## CHAPTER XII.



## CHAPTER XIII.



## CHAPTER XIV



## CHAPTER XV.

## CHAPTER XVI.



## CHAPTER XVII.



## CHAPTER XVIII.

# THE CAMEL.

---

## CHAPTER I.

### INTRODUCTORY OBSERVATIONS.

The first command addressed to man by his Creator, and substantially repeated to the second great progenitor of our race, not only charged him to subdue the earth, but gave him dominion over all terrestrial creatures, whether animate or inanimate, and thus predicted and prescribed the subjugation of the entire organic and inorganic world to human control and human use.

Man has yet by no means consummated this grand mission. He has, indeed, surveyed the greater part of his vast domain; marked the common boundary of its solid and its fluid surfaces, and approximately measured their areas and determined their relative elevation; pierced its superficial strata, and detected the order of their historical succession; reduced to their primal elements its rocks, its soils, its waters, and its atmosphere, and even soared above its canopy of cloud. He has traced, through the void of space, its movements of rotation, revolution, and translation; resolved the seeming circles of its attendant satellite into strangely tortuous paths of progression; investigated its relations of density, attraction, and motion, to other visible and invisible cosmical orbs; and unfolded the laws of those mysterious allied agencies, heat, light, electricity, and magnetism, whose sphere of influence seems commensurate with that of creation. But, notwithstanding these triumphs, earth is not yet all his own; and millions of leagues of her surface still lie uninhabited, unenjoyed, and unsubdued, yielding neither food, nor clothing, nor shelter to man, or even to the humbler tribes of animal or vegetable life, which minister to his other necessities, convenience, or enjoyments.

In like manner, we have studied the biography of organic life in its infinitely varied, and more conspicuous, contemporaneous forms, and the relations of affinity or dependence between them; traced the history of myriads of species of both plants and animals, which had ceased to be before the Creator breathed into our nostrils the breath of life; and demonstrated the past and present existence of numerous tribes of organic beings, too minute to be individually cognizable by any of the unaided senses, yet largely influencing our own animal economy, and even composing no unimportant part of the crust of the solid globe; but of the vegetables that clothe and diversify its soil, of the animated creatures that float in its atmosphere, enliven its surface, or cleave its waters, comparatively few have as yet been rendered in any way subservient to human use, fewer still domesticated and made the permanent and regular denizens of our fields or companions of our households.

The efforts of *civilized* man towards the fulfilment of this great command have been directed almost exclusively to the conquest of the *inorganic* creation, by the utilization of minerals, by contriving methods for availing himself of the mechanical powers and of natural forces, simply or in cunning combinations, by cutting narrow paths for facilitating travel and transport between distant regions, and by devising means of traversing with certainty and speed the trackless and troubled ocean.

The proper *savage* smelts no ores, and employs those metals only which natural processes have reduced. He binds the blocks of which he rears his rude temples with no cement of artificial stone. He drains no swamps, cuts no roads, excavates no canals, turns no mills by power of water or of wind, and asks from *inorganic* nature no other gifts than those which she spontaneously offers, to supply his wants and multiply his enjoyments.

But the very dawn of social life, in those stages of human existence which precede all true civilization, demands, as an indispensable condition, not the mere usufruct of the spontaneous productions of the *organic* world, but the complete appropriation and domestication of many species of both plants and animals. Man begins by subjugating, and thereby preserving, those organic forms which are at once best suited to satisfy his physical wants, and, like himself, least fitted for a self-sustaining, independent existence; and he is to end by extending his conquests over the more widely dissimilar, remote, and refractory products of creative nature. We accordingly owe to our primeval, untutored ancestors, the discovery, the domestication, the acclimatization of our cereal grains, our edible roots, our improved fruits, as well as the subjugation of our domestic animals; while civilized man has scarcely reclaimed a plant of spontaneous growth, or added a newly tamed animal to the flocks and herds of the pastoral ages. Indeed, so remote is the period to which these noble triumphs of intelligent humanity over brute and vegetable nature belong, that we know not their history or their epochs; and if we believe them to be in fact human conquests, and not rather special birthday gifts from the hand of the Creator, we must admit that cultivation and domestication have so completely metamorphosed and diversified the forms and products, and modified the habits, and even, so to speak, the inborn instincts, of both vegetables and animals, that but the fewest of our household beasts and our familiar plants can be certainly identified with the primitive stock. Most of these, it is probable, no longer occur in their wild state and original form; and it is questionable whether they are even capable of continued existence without the fostering care of man.[1]

In both these great divisions of organic life

[1] It is not the domestic animals alone, whose existence is perpetuated by the protective, though often unconscious, agency of man. In the depths of our northern forests the voice of the song-bird, or of the smaller quadrupeds, is but seldom heard. It is in the fields tilled by human husbandry that they find the most abundant nutriment, and the surest retreat from bird and beast of prey. The vast flights of the wild pigeon are found, not in the remote, primitive woodlands, but along the borders of the pioneer settlements; and, upon our western frontier, it is observed that the deer, the hare, and other feeble animals multiply for a time after the coming in of the whites, because the civilized huntsman destroys or scares away the wolf, the great natural enemy of the weaker quadrupeds, and checks the spread of the prairie fires, which often surprise their young.

there are some species peculiarly suited to the uses of man as a migratory animal. The bread-stuffs of the old world, and, in a less degree, Indian corn,[1] our only American cereal, the pulse,

[1] The cereal grains of Europe and Asia are by original constitution, or by long domestication, so thoroughly cosmopolite in their organization and habits, that they require no gradual acclimatization when transferred to new localities; and seed wheat grown in the tropics will thrive and ripen on the borders of the polar circle. Indian corn, on the contrary, either because it has been more recently reclaimed, or from some inherent physiological peculiarity, much less readily accommodates itself to new conditions. With every perceptible change of climate a new variety occurs, and it is only by a slow and gradual process of successive removals that maize originating in Virginia can be brought to maturity in New Hampshire. Upon the American continent maize is cultivated from the sea level to the height of 10,000 feet, and from the equator to at least 46° N. L. in Europe, to the height of 3,000 feet (in the Pyrenees) and as far north as 52°. The cultivation of wheat reaches the height of 4,500 feet in Europe, of 10,000 in Peru. It is grown in the vicinity of Frondhjem, in Norway, in Lat. 64°, while rye sometimes ripens three or four degrees nearer the pole. Wittiver, *Physicalische Geographie*, 510, infers from the German and Italian names of this grain, *Türkisches Korn*, *grano turco*, that it is of Asiatic origin, but this appellation evidently had its source in the geographical ignorance which in the Middle Ages so constantly confounded Turkey with India, India with America; and all historical evidence goes to show that maize is exclusively an American plant. Equally erroneous is the statement of Burmeister, *Geschichte der Schöpfung*, 23, that Indian corn was only known upon the *western* slope of

the cucurbitaceous plants, and the edible roots of our gardens, as well as the horse, the dog, the sheep, the swine, and our barnyard fowls, seem almost exempted from subjection to climatic laws. While, therefore, a degree of latitude, a few hundred feet of elevation, a trifling difference in soil, or in the amount of atmospheric humidity, oppose impassable barriers to the diffusion of most wild plants and animals, the domesticated species I have enumerated follow man in his widest wanderings, and make his resting-place their home, whether he dwells on continent or on island, at the level of the sea or on the margin of Alpine snows, beneath the equator or among the frosts of the polar circle.

Others, again, of the domesticated families of the organic world seem, like the untamed tribes, inexorably confined within prescribed geographical bounds, and incapable of propagation or growth beyond their original limits; while others still, though comparatively independent of climate and of soil, are nevertheless so specially fitted to certain conditions of surface, and to certain modes of human life, to the main-

the Cordilleras and their plateaus. It does not indeed appear that maize has been found wild in North America; but the first discoverers describe it as a plant cultivated along the whole Atlantic coast, from Massachusetts to the Gulf of Mexico.

tenance of which they are themselves indispensable, that even the infidel finds, in these mutual adaptations, proofs of the existence and beneficent agency of a self-conscious and intelligent creative power.[1]

[1] See extract from Volney, *post*.

# CHAPTER II.

## ADAPTATION OF THE CAMEL TO CERTAIN LOCAL CONDITIONS — LITERATURE OF THE SUBJECT.

AMONG the animated organisms of this latter class, the camel is, doubtless, the most important and remarkable. The Ship of the Desert[1] has

1 Wilkinson, in his Handbook for Travellers in Egypt, denies that the Orientals bestow this figurative appellation upon the camel, and affirms that its European use is founded on a misapprehension of the meaning of an Arabic term (*mrkb*) often applied to the camel, and simply signifying *vehicle*, and not properly *ship*, as it has been translated. But Sir William Jones uses the phrase in his translations of Arabic poems, and Langlès, in his Notes to Chardin, gives the corresponding Arabic words in a form, which admits of none but the old and well-established acceptation. Besides these authorities, we may cite Daumas, *Mœurs et Coutumes de l'Algérie*, 358, where another term of the same signification is given, and a poem in praise of the Desert by the celebrated Emir, Abd-el-Kader, translated in Daumas, *Les Chevaux du Sahara*, 401, in which camels are styled

> *Vaisseaux légers de la terre,*
> Plus sûrs que les vaisseaux,
> Car le navire est inconstant.

Ritter indeed, *Erdkunde*, XIII. 744, adopts Wilkinson's correction of this supposed error, and remarks, that the Arab, navigated the pathless sand-oceans of the Sahara, and of Gobi, and thus not only extended the humanizing influences of commerce and civilization alike over the naked and barbarous African and the fur-clad Siberian savage, but, by discovering the hidden wells of the waste and the islands of verdure that surround them, has made permanently habitable vast regions not otherwise even penetrable by man. The howling wilderness now harbors and nourishes numerous tribes in more or less advanced stages of culture; and the services of that quadruped, on which Rebekah journeyed to meet her spouse, and which, though neglected and despised by the polished Egyptian, constituted a principal item in the rural wealth of the father of Joseph, are as indispensa-

familiar as he was with the camel long before he became acquainted with shipping, would much more probably have reversed the figure and called the ship, the camel of the sea.

But Hammer-Purgstall, in his most learned essay, *Das Kamel*, in the *Denkschriften der Kaiserlichen Akademie der Wissenschaften*, VI. 70, observes: "The figurative name, *the Ship of the Desert*, is known, but not the opposite metonymy, by which the ship is represented as *the camel of the wide ocean waste;* so too camels are called *the clouds of the desert*, and clouds, *the camels of the sky.*" We may therefore conclude, that Wilkinson's objection to a figure of speech, which has been long current in all the languages of Europe, is without any just foundation.

ble to these races, as are those of any other animal to man in any condition of society.

The camel lives and thrives in the tropics; through almost the whole breadth of the northern temperate zone; and is even met beyond Lake Baikal in conjunction with the reindeer, with which, among some of the northern tribes, he has exchanged offices, the deer serving as a beast of the saddle, while the camel is employed only for draught or burden.[1] But his appropriate home is the desert, and it is here alone that he acquires his true significance and value, his remarkable powers being the necessary condition and sole means by which man has in any degree extended his dominion over the Libyan and the Arabian wildernesses.

"At the return of the hot season," says the acute Volney, "every thing dries up, and the dusty gray earth offers only parched and woody stems, upon which neither the horse, the ox, nor even the goat can feed. In this state of things the desert would become uninhabitable, if nature, in the gift of the camel, had not bestowed upon it an animal of a constitution as hardy and as frugal as the soil is sterile and ungrateful. No creature exhibits so marked and exclusive an adaptation to its climate, and it would seem that an intelligent will had mutually accommodated

[1] Ritter, *Erdkunde*, XIII. 662–667.

the conditions of each to those of the other. Designing the camel to inhabit regions where he could find but a scanty supply of nourishment, nature has been economical of material in his whole organization. She has not given him the fulness of form of the ox, the horse, or the elephant, but limiting him to the purely indispensable, she has bestowed upon him a small head, almost without external ears, supported by a fleshless neck. She has stripped his thighs and legs of every muscle not essential to their movements, and has furnished his dry and meagre body with only the vessels and tendons required to knit its framework together. She has supplied him with a powerful jaw to crush the hardest aliments; but that he might not consume too much, she has narrowed his stomach and made him a ruminant. She has cushioned his foot with a mass of muscle, which, sliding in mud, and ill adapted for climbing, unfits him for every soil but a dry, even, and sandy surface, like that of Arabia. She has condemned him to servitude, by refusing him all means of defence against his enemies. Possessing neither the horns of the ox, the hoof of the horse, the tusks of the elephant, nor the speed of the stag, how can he resist the attacks of the lion, the tiger, or even the wolf? Nature, therefore, to save the species from extirpation, has hidden him in the bosom of boundless deserts, whither no vegetable luxuriance attracts the beasts of the chase, and whence the more voracious animals are banished by the scarcity of their prey; and it was not till the sword of the tyrant had driven out victims from the habitable earth and chased them into the wilderness, that the camel became the slave of man. By his subjection, the most barren of soils has become a home for a portion of the human family; and such is his importance in the economy of desert life, that his extinction would involve the destruction of the whole population of those arid regions, of whose nomade existence he is the indispensable condition."

I shall have occasion hereafter to point out an error into which Volney has fallen, with respect to the exclusive adaptation of the foot to a "dry, even, and sandy surface," but in all other points his description is as accurate as it is eloquent.

In presence of the improvements of more advanced society, the camel diminishes in numbers and finally gives place to animals better suited to the wants and caprices of higher civilization. Upon good roads, other beasts of draught and burden are upon the whole more serviceable, or, to speak more accurately, more acceptable to the tastes of cultivated nations; and the ungainly camel shares in the contempt with which the humble ass, the mule, and even the ox, are regarded by the polished and the proud. Besides this, both the products and the restraints of proper agriculture are unfavorable to his full development and physical perfection. When the soil is subjugated and enclosed, and the coarse herbage and shrubbery of spontaneous growth are superseded by artificial vegetation, he misses the pungent and aromatic juices which flavor the sun-burnt grasses and wild arborescent plants that form his accustomed and appropriate diet; the confinement of hedge, and yard, and stall, are repugnant to his roving propensities and prejudicial to his health, and he is as much out of place in civilized life as the Bedouin or the Tartar. Hence the attempts to introduce him into Spain, Italy, and other European countries have either wholly failed, or met with very indifferent success; and though he still abounds in Bessarabia, the Crimea, and all the southeastern provinces of Russia, yet the rural improvements which the German colonists have introduced into those regions have tended to reduce his numbers. When the wandering Tartar becomes stationary, encloses his possessions, and converts the desert steppe into arable ground, his camels retreat before the horse, the ox, and the sheep, and retire to the wastes beyond the Don and the Volga.[1] So

[1] Schlatter, *Bruchstücke aus Reisen im südlichen Russland*, 178–9, observes, that the number of camels among the

essentially nomade indeed is the camel in his habits, that the Arab himself dismisses him as soon as he acquires a fixed habitation. The oases of the desert are very frequently without this animal, and he is not possessed by the Fellahheen of the Sinaitic peninsula, by the inhabitants of Siwah or the oasis of Jupiter Ammon, or by those who cultivate the valleys of Mount Seir.

Of the primitive races of man, known to ancient sacred and profane history, but one, the Bedouin Arab, has retained unchanged his original mode of life, and the camel alone, by those remarkable properties, which have made habitable by man regions inaccessible to the improvements of civilization, has preserved to our own times that second act in the great drama of social life, the patriarchal condition. The Arab in all his changes of faith, heathen, christian, mussulman, has remained himself immutable; and the student of biblical antiquity must thank the camel for the lively illustrations of scripture

stationary Nogai Tartars on the borders of the Sea of Azof is continually decreasing; the breeding of horses and horned cattle having proved more profitable to the families who have discarded a roving life. But the Tartars in the Northern Crimea still breed considerable numbers of these animals, because the steppes produce coarse grasses and other fodder, acceptable to the camel, though not yielding suitable nutriment for the horse or the ox.

history presented by the camp of the Ishmaelite sheikh, who is proud of his kindred with the patient Job, and who boasts himself the lineal descendant of Ibrahim el Khaleel, or Abraham, "the friend" of God.

Independently of the observations of travellers, and the numerous scientific descriptions in books of Natural History, the European literature belonging to our subject is not extensive. The most comprehensive and satisfactory history of the animal is that presented by Ritter, in a learned and laborious essay on the geographical diffusion of the camel, in the thirteenth volume of his great Description of the Earth. In this essay, Ritter has, with his usual conscientious industry, availed himself of every source of information within his reach; but has seldom cited Eastern authors. Baron Hammer-Purgstall has now, with equal erudition and diligence, treated the subject from a point of view wholly oriental. He records the titles of sixteen Arabic works specially devoted to the camel, none of which, unfortunately, exist in any European library, and gives a large mass of citations from numerous Persian and other oriental writers in prose and verse, embodying a vast amount of information, and amply illustrating the importance of this animal in the social life of all the Asiatic, and more especially the Semitic races. The published portion of this dissertation fills more than eighty quarto pages, and will be followed by a philological and lexicographical appendix, containing the texts of the Koran and those of the Scriptures referring to the camel, the proverbs applied to him or borrowed from his habits and uses, and numerous poetical descriptions, similes, and the like, drawn from the whole range of Arabic literature. The Arabic descriptive words illustrated, explained, or cited in this part of the paper, amount to nearly six thousand. The first part appeared in the 6th volume of the Memoirs of the Imperial Academy of Science at Vienna, in 1855, and the remainder is promised for the next volume. The most important remaining contribution to our knowledge of the uses of the camel is a volume entitled, *Du Dromadaire comme bête de Somme, et comme animal de Guerre*, Paris, 1853, by the late Gen. Carbuccia, which contains much valuable information, unfortunately intermixed with exaggerations that a sounder criticism would have rejected.

# CHAPTER III.

## SPECIES AND BREEDS.

NATURALISTS divide the camel into two species, the *Camelus dromedarius*, or one-humped camel of Arabia and Africa, and the *Camelus Bactrianus*, or two-humped camel of northern Asia.[1] It has been suspected that the camel of the Sahara is distinct from that of more northern Africa, which is undoubtedly of the Arabian stock, and

[1] These geographical limitations, if not strictly accurate, are nevertheless sufficiently so for general purposes. Although Höst, *Efterretninger om Marokos*, 270, saw the two-humped camel at Morocco, and individuals of this species are sometimes met in Syria, yet it is certain that he is not bred in Africa, or in the warmer regions of the Asiatic continent, but properly belongs to northern latitudes. The one-humped camel has a wider range. He is found among the Nogai Tartars, the Kirghises, and other independent Tartar tribes, and in the highlands of central Asia; he seems to bear the cold almost as well as the Bactrian, but he has in those regions neither the speed nor the powers of endurance which characterize the dromedary of the African and Arabian deserts. Although neither species probably now exists in a wild state, yet there is good reason to believe that the Bactrian was found wild at no very remote period in the desert of Gobi, where this variety probably originated. Humboldt, *Ansichten der Natur*, I. 88.

of comparatively late introduction into that continent;[1] but this conjecture does not appear to be supported by any direct historical or physiological evidence. The scientific specific designation of the one-humped camel is not well chosen.

ARABIAN, OR ONE-HUMPED CAMEL.

The term *dromas*, as applied to the camel by the ancients, was not used to indicate a *specific* dif-

1 Minutóli thinks he recognizes the head of the camel among the figures upon an obelisk at Luxor. Upon the walls of some of the smaller apartments of the great temple of Karnac are carved heads, which certainly appear to me to resemble the camel's head more closely than that of any other quadruped; and St. John, Adventures in the Libyan Desert, Chap. XII. says he found this animal among the sculptures of the temple at the oasis of Jupiter Ammon. But recent Egyptologists consider some of these figures to represent the head of the lion, others that of the giraffe, and it is certain that no part of the skeleton of the camel has been met with in the catacombs. Although it appears from Strabo, that the tribes of the desert anciently employed the camel in the transport of merchandise between Coptos and Berenice, as they do now between Cairo and Suez, yet there is abundant evidence to show that he was not used by the

ference. The *camelus dromas* was, as the etymology of the name indicates, what the proper *dromedary* is now, that is, simply a *running*, or swift camel, used chiefly or altogether for the saddle; and he might be, as he may be still, of either species, Bactrian or Arabian, though the term dromedary is seldom merited by or applied to the former of these races. In fact, any light-built, easy-paced, and swift-footed camel, of whatever species or variety, is a dromedary; though there are certain breeds, in which the slender head, tall, short body, small hump, clean limbs, and generally livelier color, which characterize the stock, have become hereditary, just as similar peculiarities of form are perpetuated in the thorough-bred hunter and race-horse.[1] In

proper Egyptians before the time of the Ptolemies, nor does he appear to have been known upon the Barbary coast until a much later period. See Ritter's essay, *Ueber die geographische Verbreitung des Kameels, Erdkunde* XIII.

[1] "Some writer, Robinson I think, declares that he could find no difference between the camel and the dromedary, except in the price of their hire; and this opinion is confirmed by the experience of many travellers, who, with the best will in the world, have in vain essayed to coax, jerk, kick, punch, thwack, and bang their beasts into an amble. But after all, I believe it is quite certain that, among the many breeds of the camel, there is one of lighter make, easier gait, and swifter pace, which is a much less fatiguing and more expeditious *mrkb* than the common animal. This is the dromedary; and in sum, any light-built, easy-paced, swift-

popular phraseology, the term dromedary has been to a considerable extent applied to designate a camel with two humps, from an erroneous supposition that the swift riding-camel, (deloul, of the Arabs; al heiri or maherry of the Sahara; haguin or hedjin of the Nubians and Egyptians,)[1] was of that species. This mistake, imputed by Ritter to Olearius, appears to have originated in a misinterpretation of a passage of Aristotle by Solinus and Theodore Gaza; and the error,

footed, and well-trained camel (to which characteristics you may, if you please, add these external marks, *videlicet*, a slender head, a short body, a small hump, and often a livelier colour,) may lawfully lay claim to that honorable appellation. That the proportion of dromedaries is not large, you may learn from an Arabian adage, which you shall find Latinized in learned Bochart, his Hierozoïcon, after this wise: *Homines sunt ut Cameli, quorum ne quidam centesimus quisque est Dromas.*—Men be as Camels, whereof not one in the hundred is a Dromedary." *The Desert*, American Whig Review, No. XCI.

[1] I have given these names in the orthography commonly used, though certainly to some extent incorrectly, by travellers. Hammer-Purgstall, *ubi supra*, 44, thinks *deloul* a mere local or corrupted name for the dromedary, but as Burckhardt heard it in Arabia, Seetzen in the Hauran, and Layard in Mesopotamia, it is at least of wide application. *Al heiri*, or *maherry*, the North-African name of the dromedary, is spelled, more properly no doubt, *mhari* or *mahari* by the French writers on Algeria, and Hammer-Purgstall corrects *haguin*, or *hedjin*, by writing the word *hádschín* (*hajéen*), or *hedschán* (*heján*).

though exposed and corrected by Gessner, three hundred years ago, and by almost every naturalist who has since described the animal, continues to influence the language, and mislead the popular opinion, of the nineteenth century.[1]

Each of the two species comprehends numerous varieties; but they do not differ from each other in size, in form, or in speed, more widely than the breeds of the common horse. Indeed, the anatomical differences between the Arabian and the Bactrian camel are so slight, that some naturalists have maintained their specific identity; and it appears to be certain that the com-

[1] It is remarkable, that the accurate Burckhardt should have fallen into this mistake in speaking of the Bactrian camel, which he calls the *dromedary*, Notes on the Bedouins and Syria, 637; though in his Travels in Nubia, 214, he properly applies the term to the swift riding-camel of the Berbers. Similar and scarcely less remarkable instances of the tenacity of error, even when almost contemporaneously exposed, may be found in the never-ending repetitions of the old fable of the *Malström*, which, in the middle of the nineteenth century, is described by Mr. Somerville, as "a whirlpool a mile and a quarter in diameter!" of Pentland's erroneous measurement of the peaks of the Bolivian Andes; and of old Hugh Peters's romance of the compression of the water at Bellows Falls, on the Connecticut. This last fiction seems to have found special favor in Germany, where it is sanctioned by the authority of Otto Berghaus and Wittwer, all of whom assert that one cannot thrust a crowbar into the water!

mon physiological test of specific difference, the incapacity, namely, of the cross to propagate, does not hold good as applied to this animal.[1] The skeletons of the two species are distinguishable, if at all, only by a slight difference of proportion; and the visceral structure being substantially the same in both,[2] the only foundation for a specific distinction appears to be in the number of humps. In the living animal, the species are readily distinguished by this outward peculiarity; and besides this obvious difference, the Bactrian is shorter limbed and much more hairy than the Arabian camel. Some writers describe the Bactrian as upon the whole smaller and weaker than the Arabian; but as others state the contrary, the difference in this respect is probably not great. It seems well settled that in countries where the two species exist together, the cross, though inferior to the dromedary in speed, is found to be a more powerful, and for general purposes, a more serviceable animal than either of the unmixed races, as possessing in a good degree the most valuable properties of both.[3]

[1] Ritter, *Erdkunde*, XIII. 659.

[2] The stomach of the Arabian camel as described by Jackson, (see chapter VI. *post*,) appears to differ considerably from that of the Bactrian dissected by Sir Everard Home.

[3] See a valuable paper, extracted from the notes of Gen-

eral Harlan, in the Report of the American Patent Office for 1853, Agriculture, p. 61. General Harlan's testimony in favor of the strength and power of endurance of the mixed breed is exceedingly strong; but he appears to undervalue the pure Bactrian, which is certainly found extremely serviceable in European and Asiatic Russia, both for draught and burden, and in those countries, at least, is almost wholly exempt from disease. Fraser, *Khorasan*, 273. Burckhardt, Notes on the Bedouins, 110, 111, speaks of the common camel of Asia Minor as bred between a Crimean (Bactrian) stud and an Arab female, and states that the Bactrian male is regularly imported from the Crimea and exclusively kept for that purpose. If, on the contrary, the dam of the mule is a Bactrian, the progeny is weak and poor, while the offspring of the cross is vicious and intractable. The cross between the Bactrian and the mule he describes as handsome but small, and with two small humps, one of which is cut off at birth to fit the animal for bearing burdens. Burckhardt's information on these points appears to have been derived at second hand, and not from personal observation. Notwithstanding the general extreme accuracy of this great traveller, and his caution in adopting hearsay testimony, I cannot but think he is mistaken, with respect to the extent to which the hybrid between the two species is found in Asia Minor, though it is undoubtedly very common in more eastwardly regions. Travellers generally have not observed the Bactrian in any part of the Turkish empire, nor am I aware of any reliable authority for the practice of amputating one of the humps. Although, therefore, the Bactrian may have been formerly imported into Asia Minor as a breeder, I do not think he is now found, except in rare cases, in that country; and the hybrids, if any such exist there, are probably brought from Bokhara or the Persian provinces.

# CHAPTER IV.

## GENERAL ANATOMY — THE HUMP — THE HEAD, AND THE CALLOSITIES.

THE general anatomy of the camel is the same as that of other ruminants; but the hump, the horizontal posture of the head, the direction of the eye, the power of closing the nostril, the callosities upon the breast and legs, the spreading and cushioned feet, and above all the curious structure of the stomach, to which he owes his most valuable property, the power of long abstinence from water, distinguish him from all other quadrupeds.

The following account of his general anatomical structure is abridged from the English Cyclopædia, Natural History, vol. I.

"The camels have thirty-four teeth; sixteen in the upper jaw; namely, two incisors—for the camels and the llamas have these, and form the exceptions, the other ruminants being without any incisors in the upper jaw—two canines, twelve molars; eighteen in the lower jaw, namely, six incisors, two canines, and ten molars.

There is another difference between the camels and other ruminants; the former have the scaphoid and cuboid bones of the tarsus separated. Instead of the great horny case, or shoe, which envelops all the lower part of each toe, and determines the figure of the ordinary cloven hoof, the camels have only a small one, or rather the rudiment of one, adhering only to the last joint of the toe, and symmetrical in form, like the hoofs of the *Pachydermata.* These and other peculiarities of form lead to the opinion that the camels and the llamas form the link between the *Ruminantia* and the *Pachydermata.*"

"The characters of the genus may be thus summed up: Lower incisors in the form of cutting wedges; upper incisors sub-lateral; canines conical, sub-erect, strong; false molars situated in the interdentary space on either side; head long; upper lip cleft; nostrils slit obliquely; eyes prominent; ears small; neck elongated; back with fleshy bosses or hunches; tail moderate; toes united below; teats ventral, four in number; hair inclining to woolly; callosities on the breast and flexible points of the extremities; the upper lip of the camel swollen, and divided. The projecting orbits of its eyes, the lengthened and certainly not graceful neck, the back bossed with a hump or humps, and croup comparatively weak, supported on the long and awkward looking legs terminating in apparently disproportioned feet, are not materials for producing elegance of form; and indeed the air of the animal is altogether grotesque; but this uncouth shape is one of those admirable examples of contrivance, which must strike the most careless observer."

The hump is simply a fleshy or rather fatty protuberance upon the back, like that of the bison, unsupported by any special bony process, and it is least developed in the highest bred animals, so that the mahari of the Sahara is popularly described as being without that appendage. The fulness of the protuberance, however, depends much upon the condition of the animal. The state of the hump is a test constantly referred to in the sale or hire of the camel, and the jockeys resort to various contrivances to give it an unnatural plumpness and solidity.[1] When the camel has been, for a length of time, full fed, and subjected to moderate labor only, the hump assumes a greater plumpness of form and hardness of texture; but if ill kept or overworked, the fat of the hump is absorbed, the protuberance becomes flaccid, and it is sometimes even reduced to little more than its skin. It undoubt-

[1] The camel-dealers perforate the skin, and blow up the hump of the living animal, as dishonest butchers do their meat, to make it look full. Tavernier, I. 132.

edly serves as a repository of nutriment, and the absorption of its substance into the general system appears to be one of the special arrangements by which the camel is so admirably fitted for the life of privation to which he is destined.

According to Burckhardt,[1] when the animal is in the best possible case, in which condition he is only found among the richer nomade Arabs, and even there but rarely, the hump is of a pyramidal shape, covers nearly the whole back, and its length is not less than one fourth of that of the entire body. Of all the members it is last exhausted and last fattened. In long journeys it slowly wastes away, and a repose of three or four months is required to restore it to its full volume. The Arabic language has at least thirty words descriptive of the conditions of the hump, with reference to its dimensions, its fatness or leanness, its solidity or flaccidity, and the causes of all these different states of this important appendage.

The head of the camel, especially of those of the Bishari and Ababdeh breeds, is carried high and nearly horizontal; and this circumstance, with the length and curvature of the neck, and the outline of the arched back, create between the camel and the ostrich a resemblance strong

[1] Bedouins, 264.

enough abundantly to justify the name of *struthio-camelus*, which the Roman naturalists, and that of *camel-bird*, which, according to Niebuhr, the Arabs apply to that gigantic fowl.[1] But notwithstanding this horizontal bearing of the brow and front, the camel is but an apparent exception to the limitation which permits man alone *cælum tueri*. For though he seems *erectos ad sidera tollere vultus*, the structure of the skull and the position of the eye forbid an upward glance. The eye is projecting, sheltered above by a salient bony arch, and its axis is nearly parallel to that of the head, though with a slight inclination towards it anteriorly. From this conformation of the organ, the sight of the animal is habitually directed rather downwards than forward, to the ground upon which he is just about to tread than to the distance. It is, in a great degree, to this structure, as I believe, that his remarkable sure-footedness is to be attributed. The eye always scans the surface where the foot is next to be placed; and in moving about among the scattered luggage and furniture of a camp, he

1 "The ostrich himself seems to have a dim consciousness that he is a sort of equivocal middle-thing between a volatile and a quadruped, for when they said to him, fly! he answered, 'I cannot, I am a camel;' when they said, carry! he replied, 'I cannot, I am a bird.'"

*From the unpublished Journal of a Traveller in the East.*

rarely treads on the smallest article. The nostrils are fringed with long hairs, and provided with sphincters, which enable the animal to close them, and thus to exclude insects and the sand with which the desert winds are so often charged, while the hairs, to a considerable extent, perform the same office during the occasional partial opening of the apertures, required for respiration. The Bedouins understand the value of a wide nostril as well as a Newmarket jockey, and they frequently slit the nose of the animal in such a way as to give each aperture the form of a Y. The slitting of the nostrils is a common preparation for a race; and I once saw this absurd operation performed upon a dozen young dromedaries, which were to contend for the prize on the following day.

The camel is provided with seven callosities, which receive the shock of his fall in lying down for repose, or at the command of his master for the convenience of mounting and dismounting, loading and unloading, and the weight of the body is supported by them when at rest. One of these is upon the breast nearly between the fore legs, two upon each of the fore and one upon each of the hinder legs. The callosities upon the breast and at the knees are evidently organic, as they consist of a horny substance and are found in the fœtus. The others appear to be a mere thickening of the skin, and they may be the effect of friction and pressure. The full development of the callosities is one of the "points" of a good mahari, and it ought to be accompanied with a slender barrel, so that in the recumbent posture the belly shall scarcely touch the ground.

In lying down the animal throws himself slightly forward, and first bending one fore leg, poises himself for an instant, and then falls suddenly upon the callosities at the knees; he now advances the hind feet a little, and drops upon the gambrel joint; the callus upon the breast is brought to the ground by a third descent, and those upon the upper and forward part of the hind leg by a fourth. Each of these movements, (which are reversed in rising,) and especially the first, is attended with a considerable shock; and the inexperienced rider is apt to be thrown over the camel's head, unless he steadies himself by holding fast to the saddle pins. The Arabs slide down from and climb up to the saddle, without making the animal kneel, or even stopping him, and any active man may readily learn to do the same, but Europeans seldom practise this method.[1] The French soldiers in Algeria use a long

[1] Burckhardt, *Syria*, 445, remarks, that it tires the camel to lie down and rise again, and he advises the traveller to acquire the habit of mounting and dismounting while his

stirrup with two *steps* to mount by; and a loop upon a lance, such as were used by some ancient mounted troops, or attached to a musket, might answer the same purpose.

beast is standing. The Arabs often manifest impatience, when a traveller makes his camel kneel too frequently.

## CHAPTER V.

### THE FOOT.

THE foot of the camel is equally adapted to treading upon yielding sand and to climbing the rugged rock, which, in all extensive deserts, forms a much larger proportion of the surface than accumulations of sand. The surface of the wilderness is in general a hard, compact, gravelly soil, or composed of loose stones, or bare rocks, furrowed by deep and abrupt ravines; and most known deserts are apparently of submarine formation.

The foot is composed of two long toes united by and resting upon an elastic cushion with a tough and horny sole or facing. The foot spreads upon touching the ground somewhat like that of the moose and reindeer, and affords a broader support to the weight of the animal than almost any other quadruped is provided with. The camel, therefore, sinks less in the sand than any other large animal; but he nevertheless instinctively avoids it, as a horse does a puddle, and prefers any other surface except mud, loose rolling pebbles, and sharp-pointed rocks. Burckhardt[1] observes: "It is an erroneous opinion, that the camel delights in sandy ground. It is true, that he crosses it with less difficulty than any other animal, but wherever the sands are deep, the weight of himself and his load makes his feet sink into them at every step, and he groans and often sinks under his burden." Denham and Clapperton say their camels sometimes sank almost knee-deep in the loose sand, and that, in descending steep sand-hills, they were so helpless as to require their drivers to support them and keep them from falling forwards by holding them back by the tail.[2]

The sole, though of a horny texture, is sufficiently yielding to allow the cushion of the foot to accommodate itself to the inequalities of a rocky surface,[3] and the camel climbs with facility ascents so steep and rugged, or even so slippery, as to be scaled with difficulty by any other domestic animal. The limestone ledges in the northern portion of the lesser Arabian peninsula

[1] Syria, 622.

[2] Denham and Clapperton's Travels, I. chap. 3, do. p. 169. Pietro della Valle complains that his camel, though the freshest and strongest in the caravan, fell in the soft sand "more than seven times in one day."

[3] The sole seems entirely impenetrable to thorns, and the camel treads with impunity on the strong sharp spines with which the fallen branches of the desert acacias are thickly armed.

are often worn to a glassy smoothness by primitive water currents, or by the attrition of the desert sands, yet the camel traverses them in all directions with entire security. Observing a caravan climb a long ascent of this description in Arabia Petræa, I had the curiosity to measure the inclination of the rock, and found the angle with the horizon to be fifteen degrees. The surface was everywhere almost as slippery as polished marble, and the length of the slope exceeded half a mile; but the whole caravan of more than fifty camels surmounted it without any accident. The northern slope of the pass of Negabad, on the eastern arm of the Red Sea, appears to me even steeper than that I have just described, and the path is as rugged and the zigzags as short as those of almost any of the mule routes over the Alps, but it is constantly crossed by loaded caravans without difficulty. But these are trifles compared with the performances of camels in Algeria, as stated by the French officers. According to an official report to the war department of France in 1844, in the expedition to Milianeh, camels carrying burdens of 250 kilogrammes (550 pounds) climbed without accident slopes rising at an angle of forty-five degrees, and readily traversed every route practicable by mules.[1]

[1] Carbuccia, *Du Dromadaire*, pp. 8, 169.

Although the Arabian camel traverses the roughest routes and climbs exceedingly steep ascents, yet the Bactrian and the cross between the two species are even better fitted for scaling difficult mountain passes. This difference is, probably, partly due to habit and training; but the greater elongation of the toe of these breeds, which sometimes projects beyond the cushioned sole and forms a sort of claw, undoubtedly somewhat facilitates climbing by giving a grasp to the foot-hold, for which reason the Bactrian anciently was, and sometimes still is, called the mountain camel.

My Russian correspondents, to whom I have so often referred, say that the Bactrian is chiefly used for winter transportation, and that his feet require no protection, but, to use their own words, are so formed that he travels well not only on frozen ground, but upon ice and snow.[1] Timkowski saw caravans of this breed cross a glacier; and Bergmann says that, in winter, the Calmucks prefer them to horses for the saddle, because their long legs enable them to wade through

[1] Carbuccia, p. 10, speaks of the use of leather shoes to protect the foot of the camel on rocky ground, and it appears from Hammer-Purgstall's Essay, p. 30, that wrappages of leather are applied to the foot in Arabia as a defence against the cold, which would otherwise crack or split the horny sole.

deeper snows. General Harlan conducted a train of two thousand camels of the mixed breed a distance of three hundred and sixty miles, "over the snow-clad summits of the Indian Caucasus," in winter, with the loss of but a single camel, and even that one was killed by an accident unconnected with disease or fatigue, though the campaign lasted seven months.

The structure of the foot gives the animal a peculiarly silent tread. The thunder which at a distance announces the approach of a troop of cavalry, does not herald the advance of a caravan; and with high-bred maharis, whose voice does not betray the march of a foraging party, the Bedouin may surprise the most watchful enemy.

In mud, the footing of the camel is insecure. The hind legs are little separated down to the gambrel joint, but from this point they diverge at a considerable angle, so that an ancient Arabic poem compares the hinder feet to two water-buckets borne upon a yoke, and the increased breadth of base thus acquired contributes much to the sure-footedness of the camel on dry ground.

Upon a wet and slippery soil, on the contrary, the liability of the foot to slide is increased by this arrangement; and in case of such an accident, as the foot usually slides laterally, the hip joint is often dislocated or so badly wrenched that the animal is unable to rise with his burden and proceed upon his journey.[1] It is commonly said that the camel never rises after falling under his load, and that he immediately perishes under such circumstances. I have myself witnessed instances to the contrary, although I have no doubt that when the fall is from *exhaustion*, the death of the animal is nearly certain. Where the mud is merely a thin layer of wet earth over a rocky or other very hard surface, the camel

[1] According to General Harlan, the hind legs are sometimes hoppled above the gambrel joint to prevent their spreading on wet ground. "But as touching this matter of security I must put in a *caveat*. I will be responsible for the sure-footedness of the camel on dry soils only; for if there be mud, water running or stagnant, or even if the ground be damp enough to run a western steamboat, travellers agree that the Arabian camel is very apt to come down unhandsomely; his forefoot slipping and wringing his withers, or his hind legs spreading and dislocating, or sorely wrenching his hip joints. Tavernier says the same thing even of the Turcoman camel, accustomed as he is to rain and snow; and goes so far as to affirm that the drivers spread carpets over wet places for their beasts to tread upon. I have often seen camels slip, but never fall, in the mud; and I have not observed that they were particularly shy of wet, as some authors declare. On the contrary, in passing along the beach of the Red Sea, in the Gulf of Akaba, my dromedary fairly took to the water, and I had to use some very energetic persuasives to induce him to return to *terra firma*." *The Desert.*

passes over it without much risk; and I have repeatedly seen caravans travel at their ordinary pace and with entire confidence and security over pavements covered with several inches of snow and soft mud.

The camel readily fords rivers with gravelly or pebbly bottoms. Tavernier remarks, that between Alexandretta and Baïas, where the road runs along the sea-shore, the camels are obliged in many places to pass through the water around projecting points, and I have seen them wade around headlands in the Red Sea, in water three or four feet deep; but the passage of streams with soft bottoms, or with deep water, by camels, is always a matter of some difficulty. It is not easy to train them to enter a ferry-boat, or to lie quietly in crossing rivers by this mode of conveyance; and though they float readily, yet they are bad swimmers, the roundness of the barrel and the height of the head and hump above the line of flotation exposing them constantly to the danger of losing their balance and rolling over upon the side, in which case they are sure to be lost. For this reason it is common to lash the head to the gunwale of a boat, or to support it by some other contrivance in crossing deep waters. Denham and Clapperton saw them guided in crossing rivers, by a man swimming before them and holding the halter in his teeth, and they observe that the camel of the Sahara is often seized with illness after swimming, and dies in a few hours. Lyon says their drivers hold up their heads in the water by the upper lip, and that sometimes a man sits behind the hump, to depress the croup, and elevate the head. Burckhardt mentions the practice of tying inflated goat-skins to their necks to aid them in swimming.

But although Father Huc, whose lively imagination serves to magnify all things, encountered almost insurmountable difficulties in crossing streams with Tartar camels, it appears that the Bactrian finds the frigid and bridgeless rivers of Siberia no very serious obstacles to his progress.

Pallas saw Bactrian camels used "as leaders," in the conveyance of the post and of travellers through half-frozen morasses near Lake Baikal, and he observes that they ford the most rapid torrents. An older traveller, Yobrand Ides, describes them as loth to enter a torrent, but says, that if they are swept off their legs by the violence of the current, "no creature swims more easily." It appears, however, by his account, that it is rather floating than swimming, for he states that the animal makes little voluntary effort, and his movements are wholly directed by his driver, who swims before and guides the train by the halter.

# CHAPTER VI.

## ANATOMY OF THE STOMACH.

THE most interesting and important anatomical peculiarity of the camel is that curious structure by which he is enabled to take in at once, and by a special arrangement retain, a sufficient quantity of water to supply the wants of the animal economy for several days. It was conjectured by Cuvier, and it is believed by some more recent naturalists, that the stomach of the camel is not only able to retain for many days water swallowed by the animal, but that it possesses the further power of secreting a special fluid for moistening the fauces and viscera, and mingling with the food in rumination, in some such way as some fish are able to keep the skin moist for some time after they are taken from the water, by the exudation of a fluid secreted for that purpose. It is even said that the fluid found in the water-sac, after the death of the camel, possesses chemical properties which prove it to be an animal secretion; but it does not appear that this fact has been established to the satisfaction of the physiological chemist.[1]

It is not easy to explain the structure of the stomach without drawings, but the following clear and detailed account of the anatomy of that organ in the Arabian camel, from a paper by Dr. Jackson, in the fourth volume of the Boston Journal of Natural History, will prove intelligible to all, and especially interesting to physiological inquirers. Dr. Jackson, dissected both the male and female of this species, and noticed some remarkable deviations from the structure of the stomach of the Bactrian, as represented by Sir Everard Home. I give Sir E. Home's somewhat confused description in an appendix to this volume, for the purpose of comparison.

"The stomach of the female consisted of three cavities. The first, or the *paunch*, was of a rounded form, about two or two and a half feet in diameter, and nearly filled with food, which was unchanged and for the most part dryish, though in the depending parts there was a little water. The inner surface was formed by a white, thin, dense, wrinkled cutis without papillæ, and lined by a delicate cuticle. The muscular coat was strongly developed, the fibres generally extending from the cardiac orifice to the opposite extremity of the organ, so as to force up the con-

[1] Carbuccia, p. 16.

tents towards the œsophagus in the process of rumination, the cud being evidently returned into the mouth from this cavity, and not from the second, as in the bullock; there was also a thin layer passing in an opposite direction, besides some irregular fibres which would give a rotatory movement to the contents. The most efficient muscular power, however, was a large thick band in the posterior parietes; it was eighteen inches in length, arose near the cardiac orifice, around which it communicated with the small band which went to the second cavity, and was at this part six inches broad; at the thickest part, midway, it was an inch and a quarter in width, and at the further extremity it became broader, thinner, and was gradually lost in the parietes."

"The cells in the *first* cavity, which serve the animal as a reservoir for water, were arranged in two rows. The first extended fifteen inches from the orifice of the second cavity, along the posterior parietes, towards the left side. Ten transverse and parallel septa were sent off at a right angle from the strong muscular band, varying in length from five to nine inches, and in depth from three fourths to more than two inches, but becoming less and less marked towards the left side, where they gradually disappear. These septa are intersected by others which are thinner, for the most part quite regular, and situated about one inch apart, thus forming the cells which, by estimate, would hold generally from one to four ounces; at the left extremity, where these last septa are most deficient, the cells are very large, one of them measuring five and a half by two inches, and being capable of holding not far from three or four gills. The first-named transverse septa are from two to four lines thick on their free edge, in which are seen well-developed muscular fibres arising directly from the large band in the posterior parietes of the organ, though less strongly marked than they are represented by Sir E. Home; his figure, however, was taken from the two-humped camel and not from the dromedary; the cells, also, are surrounded by a few irregular fibres, which would tend to expel their contents. In order to see the fibres in any part of this cavity, the cutis had to be dissected away. The second row of cells commenced about opposite the middle of the first row on the right side, and extended thirty-four inches round towards the front of the organ. There were nine transverse septa, from three to five inches in length, quite regular at the anterior extremity, but much less so posteriorly; the largest were two and a half inches apart. Midway they formed large continuous cells, capable of holding eight ounces or more; anteriorly, they were intersected by other septa, forming very regular cells, which would have held from two to four ounces, but posteriorly the cells were very irregular, holding about two ounces."

"The *second* cavity of the stomach, which must serve merely as a receptacle for water, had a crescentic form, the small curvature measuring seven inches, and the large, fifteen. It communicated very freely with the first cavity at the distance of four and one-half inches from the œsophagus: the opening into the third cavity is smaller, and immediately below this it formed a cul-de-sac which was two inches deep; midway, it measured, transversely, on the inner surface, nine and a half inches. In the small curvature there was a smooth space, four inches wide at the left extremity, but diminishing to one inch at the right. Along this space there ran a strongly marked muscular band; it arose on the left side of the termination of the œsophagus, measured there one inch wide, but gradually diminished and terminated at the opening of the second cavity into the third. Thus the opening of the third cavity is drawn up towards that of the œsophagus to receive the cud that has been chewed, and which is prevented from falling again into the first cavity by the united action of the large muscular band in the first cavity, and the small one in the second. The cells of this cavity were much more numerous, and very much smaller than those of the first, with which they were almost directly continuous; on an average they would have held from three to four drams, but the largest, which was situated at the left extremity, were from two to four times as large. There were thirteen transverse septa, counting them on the large curvature, but some of these bifurcated and some united towards their extremities. These were intersected by two others, four or five inches long and one fourth of an inch wide, which arose from the left extremity of the cavity, ran parallel along the large curvature and were gradually lost; they were also intersected by very numerous, short, but not continuous septa, which formed the cells. This cavity, like the first, was lined by cutis, without papillæ; cuticle not raised. Muscular coat about two lines thick; fibres mostly longitudinal, though some were transverse; the same structure was also seen about the cells and in the septa."

"The *third* cavity, or true organ of digestion, was for the most part thin and membranous, of an elongated form, but somewhat incurvated, and measured three and a half feet in length. Being cut open, it measured three inches across at the left extremity, fourteen inches at the largest part, or about the junction of the first and second thirds, eight inches where it became contracted, or at the distance of six inches from the pylorus, after which it dilated to twelve inches, and then contracted again at the pylorus, to four and a half inches. This cavity at the left extremity was of about a uniform size throughout the first five inches, but there was not the slightest appearance of a separate cavity as generally described, and as is strongly represented by Home in the Bactrian camel; otherwise the form of this third cavity corresponded perfectly with his figure. He remarks upon the intermediate cavity as so small that it might be overlooked, were it not for the distinctness of its orifices; but this last was not found in either of the individuals under description. He remarks, also, upon the absence of septa and of the cuticle which generally characterize the third cavity of ruminants, and which absence, in the present case, seemed to be a strong additional reason for denying the existence of an intermediate cavity. The mucous membrane generally was smooth, soft, extremely thin, and thrown into loose longitudinal folds, of which there were counted about forty, commencing towards the left extremity, where the dilatation began, and terminating within six inches of the pylorus; in it were some small mucous follicles. Upon the inner surface of that portion of the left extremity which is generally described as an additional cavity, were seen the faint remains of cells, which passed imperceptibly into the plicæ. Sir E. Home remarks, upon "a faint appearance of a honey-combed structure, so slight as to require a close inspection to ascertain it." In the last six inches of the pyloric portion, the structure of the lining membrane was entirely changed. The greater part had the soft villous appearance of mucous coat, but was much thickened. The remainder, situated in the large curvature, and to the extent of about six inches square, was about one line in thickness, and very peculiar in structure, consisting of fine, upright, parallel fibres, easily separated from each other, and from the subjacent parts; the surface was smoother than that of the surrounding mucous coat, though thrown into very thick and strongly marked rugæ. Just at the pylorus was the glandular body, as it is described in the camel and bullock by Home; it was about one inch broad, and about one half inch thick, from which place it extended backwards along the small curvature, and was gradually lost in the parietes; it was covered by mucous membrane, and consisted of a soft, white tissue, without any glandular appearance. The pylorus was well marked, though not very prominent. The muscular coat of this cavity was quite thick, especially at the rugous part, the fibres being transverse."

"The stomach of the *male* corresponded mainly with the above description. In the first cavity, the cells on the left side extended fourteen inches; there were ten transverse septa, four and a half to nine inches long, three fourths of an inch to two inches apart, and intersected, though not regularly, by short septa; three or four of the cells would probably have held eight or ten ounces. The cells on the right side commenced about opposite the middle of the large muscular band, and were thirty-nine inches in extent; thirteen transverse septa; cells midway about three inches wide and very shallow, but at each extremity much smaller. The muscular band was twenty-two inches long, and midway one half inch thick. Small curvature of the second cavity eight and one half inches, and the large, ten and one half; inner surface midway and transversely, ten and one half inches; twelve transverse septa, more regular than in the female, the two large ones which intersected them running about half the length of the cavity; cells would have held from half an ounce to an ounce; small muscular band seventeen inches long, one inch wide, and about two lines thick; muscular coat generally thick, and the fibres transverse, being in the female mostly longitudinal. Third cavity forty inches long. Measured transversely at the left extremity, three inches, diminishing afterwards to two and three fourths, but without any appearance of there being an intermediate cavity; at the largest part it was fourteen inches, at the contracted part nine, at the largest part, after it again dilated, nineteen, and at the pylorus four inches. There were about forty or fifty longitudinal plicæ; beyond these the lining membrane was about half a line thick, firm and rough on the surface, and there was seen the peculiar rugous membrane that was described in the female, except that the color here was cineritious. The gland at the pylorus, as it has been called, was two inches long, one inch wide, and half an inch thick."

It has often been said, that when desert travellers are reduced to extremity by thirst, their camels are killed for the sake of the water to be found in their stomachs. In a note to Russell's History of Aleppo, the editor remarks, "That water, in cases of emergency, is taken from the stomach of camels, is a fact neither doubted in Syria nor thought strange. I never was myself in a caravan reduced to such an expedient, but I had the less reason to distrust the report of others, particularly of the Arabs, seeing that even the love of the marvellous could in such a case be no inducement to invention. It may, perhaps, be superfluous to produce the authority of an Arab historian, (Beidaw), who, in his account of the Prophet's expedition to Tabuc against the Greeks, relates, among other distresses of the army, that they were reduced to the necessity of killing their camels for the sake of the water contained in their stomachs." Daubenton found in the stomach of a camel which had been dead ten days, about three pints of clear water, almost tasteless and still drinkable. Carbuccia states, § 16, that the stomach of a dead camel opened in Algeria, in the presence of several officers, was found to contain more than fifteen litras of a greenish fluid, of a not unpleasant taste. The Arabs who were present said that after standing three days the water would become clear and drinkable, and the experiment was tried with success. Capt. Lyon asserts that water is taken from the stomach of the camel, strained and drunk. Although, therefore, Burckhardt[1] declares that he never heard of killing the camel for the water in the reservoir, and doubts whether that fluid would be found in it, the fact that under some circumstances water in considerable quantities is found in the stomach, must be regarded as established. But a case would not be likely to occur where the supply would not hold out as long in the water-skins of the traveller as in the stomach of the camel, and therefore the necessity of a resort to this source must be extremely rare.

[1] Bedouins, 260.

## CHAPTER VII.

### SIZE, COLOR, DISEASES, TEMPER, AND LONGEVITY.

THE height and bulk of the camel are very different in different breeds. The average height of the Arabian camels I have measured was nineteen hands, or six feet four inches to the top of the hump, the head being an inch or two higher.[1] The tallest I have used measured seven feet, and seven feet three inches respectively. The very powerful Turcoman camel is said to be somewhat lower than the Arabian; but the individuals of this breed, composing two large caravans, I saw at Broussa and near Ghemlih, were taller than the Arabian camels I have seen, by from four to six inches. The height of the Bactrian is stated at from six to eight and a half

[1] Hammer-Purgstall, in commenting on a passage of an Arabic poem, which he translates, "She lowered her head to the level of the saddle," observes that the head of the camel is much higher than his saddle. This may be true of the saddle of the mahari, which is placed on the withers, but not of the pack-saddle, or the common dromedary saddle used in Arabia.

feet, his weight at one third more than that of the ox, which, in the Crimea, is estimated at nine hundred pounds, thus making the weight of the camel twelve hundred. The Bactrians kept at the Jardin des Plantes, and described by Cuvier, measured about seven feet five inches to the withers. If this measurement wholly excludes the forward hump, which is sometimes nearly two feet in height, the stature of the animal must be very considerably above the average of that of the Arabian. I was informed at Pisa, that the animals of the Grand Duke's stables sometimes came up to fourteen hundred English pounds, but I doubt the accuracy of the information.

The swift dromedary varies even more in size than the burden camel. Layard,[1] mentions a deloul from the Nedjd, where very fine animals are raised, which was little taller than an Arab horse, and all the proper Arabian dromedaries I have seen were very small. The hajéen of the Upper Nile, on the contrary, is much taller, frequently, I am sure, not below eight feet. Lyon speaks of a Tibboo mahari of seven feet eight inches as small;[2] and on one occasion a dromedary of this variety, measuring not less than

[1] New Researches, 332.

[2] Lyon's Travels in Africa, 313.

nine feet and a half to the middle of the back, was brought to the camp of Denham.[1]

The most common colors of the camel are mouse, drab, fawn, brown, and black. The Nubian is, however, generally white, and the same color not unfrequently occurs in the Bactrian. Brown, according to Burckhardt, is disliked; the reddish or light gray, which sometimes occurs, is preferred by the Anezeh ladies, while black is the fashionable color with the women of Nedjd. I have seen two or three instances of a very delicate and pleasing rose tint, and these appeared to be favorite animals. The color is always, so far as I have observed, nearly uniform, except that the parts least exposed are commonly lighter, and the long hair about the neck and hump a few shades darker, than the rest of the fleece. Spotted, striped, or mottled camels, I have never seen.

Gen. Harlan thinks the cross between the Bactrian and the Arabian more subject to disease than the horse, but observes, that in this respect he has "greatly the advantage of the dromedary of the plains, which frequently die in great numbers, without apparent cause, especially during the rainy season." At this season, particularly, the camels are subject to an epilepsy or other convulsion, which is frequently fatal. Confinement and uncleanliness expose them to

[1] Denham and Clapperton, I. 169.

mange, which, if neglected, produces death. Burckhardt mentions as diseases always fatal, a paralysis and distortion of the neck, probably the "convulsion" noticed by Harlan, a diarrhœa which attacks the young, and a colic caused by swallowing with their fodder the dried dung of goats or sheep. When broken-winded, which is of frequent occurrence, they are treated with the cautery, a favorite remedy among most rude tribes; and a wounded hump, or a galled back, is relieved by the same means. I have seen several instances of serious inconvenience from an annoyance mentioned by Burckhardt, the drawing up of leeches into the mouth while drinking. The leeches attach themselves to the back of the palate and the gums, and often make a lodgment under the tongue. The inaccessibility of the parts, and the impatience of the camel, render the removal of these pests difficult, and the animal is often sensibly weakened by the loss of blood, while the soreness of the mouth produced by the puncture of the leech, prevents him from feeding freely. Carbuccia treats at considerable length of the maladies of the camel, their causes, and remedies. The most formidable of these causes appears to be the sting, or more probably the oviposition of a gad-fly, which gives rise to a multitude of diseases. Starvation, which Carbuccia judiciously classes among "fatal maladies," is declared to follow next after the sting of the *debab*, as a source of mortality. The panacea for most diseases, and even for the frenzy of the male at the rutting season, is an external application of *tar*, not that extracted from the pine, which is said to have no medicinal properties, but yielded by a native African plant called *arar*, or *tâga*.

The general testimony of observers is, that the Arabian camel is liable to fewer diseases than most domestic animals; but the experience of Burckhardt, of Harlan, and of Carbuccia, certainly strongly tends to show that this opinion is not altogether sound. With the Bactrian, however, the case is certainly otherwise; and it is abundantly shown that, at least in favorable localities, he enjoys an almost complete exemption from the numerous maladies to which the one-humped camel is subject. In reply to special inquiries on this point, I am informed that almost the only disease occurring among the Bactrians, in Bessarabia, is a blistering of the tongue occasioned by bad or decayed fodder, and sleeping on damp and dirty ground. The soreness of the tongue prevents the animal from eating, and he pines away. The only known remedy is the actual cautery.

In connection with the hygiene of the camel, I may mention the furious excitement of the male at the rutting season, which amounts to a positive malady. It lasts through a period of some weeks, during which he hardly tastes food; and Tavernier even affirms that he neither eats nor drinks for forty days. At this time he is ungovernable, violent, and revengeful, to that degree that his master or others sometimes fall victims to his rage. Carbuccia declares, as before noticed, that the paroxysm may be calmed by tarring the head of the animal. Castration is attended with the same general results and advantages as in the case of other quadrupeds, and it may be performed, it is said, at any age, and without risk to the animal, or even a temporary loss of his services. Various methods are employed, among which puncturing the testes with a sharp red-hot iron is recommended as the best.

The period of gestation does not appear to be uniform. At least, most travellers state it at a year for cold climates, while some declare that the period varies from ten or eleven months to a year in warmer ones. Alfred von Kremer even informs us, that a ten month's foal is preferred in Egypt to one of longer gestation. The female bears every second year, and always a single foal. She is used during pregnancy and lactation, at least in hot countries, though in colder climates she is generally allowed to repose for a part at least of the former period. Harlan thinks that "the female of neither race is of much value for burden," and Burckhardt says she is inferior to the male in strength, but is considered both swifter and better able to support thirst.

It is not easy to learn much from the Arabs respecting the *periods* in the biography of the camel. "Few Bedouins know their own age or that of their children, and they cannot be expected to possess a better acquaintance with the chronology of their cattle." The age at which he becomes serviceable varies with breed, climate, and other circumstances, but in general he is put to labor in his third year, and arrives at his full strength earlier or later in his fourth. His longevity is more uncertain. In India, according to Forbes, he lives but twenty-five years. In Algeria, he does not attain a greater age than thirty years, and he is fit for labor from fifteen to twenty. In Syria and Asia Minor, his ordinary life and service are ten years longer. A correspondent in Bessarabia estimates the average life of the Bactrian in that province at thirty-five years; while a Russian officer, of much experience in the use of this animal in the Crimea, assures me that he lives ordinarily to the age of sixty or seventy, and sometimes even to a hundred. In any event, it is well settled that his term of life and period of useful service very considerably exceed those of the horse.

The camel, though less vicious than the horse, is not altogether so patient an animal as he is generally represented. His anger is indeed not easily excited, but when once thoroughly irritated, he long remembers the injury which has provoked him; and the "camel's temper" is a proverbial expression used by the Arabs to denote a vindictive and unforgiving disposition.[1] Although he sometimes strikes with the fore foot, yet the hoof being unarmed, his blows are feeble, and his only dangerous weapon is his teeth. These are used with powerful effect in the barbarous fights which are sometimes got up as spectacles,[2] but it is only under certain special circumstances, which are easily avoided, that he attacks his driver.

His only ordinary manifestation of discontent, is the harsh and ill-natured growl he sets up whenever he is approached to be loaded or mounted, and especially when any attempt is made to overcharge him. In the stillness of the desert, the growl of a caravan, preparing for the morning's march, is heard for miles around; though the true mahari seldom growls, and it is

1 Höst, an accurate observer, says, (*Efterretninger om Marokos*, 269,) that the Sultan of Morocco had camels trained to act as executioners.

2 Macfarlane describes one of these cruel exhibitions, at Smyrna, as a very savage and repulsive scene.

said there are breeds which have entirely lost this disagreeable peculiarity; yet, in general, silent as is the march of a burden caravan, its halts are very unmistakably announced to all wanderers within a long distance of its track.[1] So harsh indeed is the growl of the camel, that Father Huc[2] gravely declares that his camel-driver, on one occasion, put a pack of wolves to flight by tweaking his camel's nose till he roared again.

The dentition of the camel, like that of other domestic quadrupeds, furnishes a convenient indication of the age of the animal up to twelve years, when it is completed, and no longer serves as a criterion. I do not find a description of the growth of the teeth during the first five years, but Burckhardt says that, at the beginning of the sixth year, the first pair of back teeth appear, early in the eighth the second pair, and in the tenth the third, each pair taking two years for its growth.

I will close this chapter of disagreeables by an extract from a writer whom I have often quoted.

"But on this head of *désagremens* I do not care to be diffuse; and I will mention as one of

[1] "Muzzle the mouths of your camels, and when they are reposing, avoid approaching them, lest the groans they would utter at the sight of their masters rouse the enemy. Daumas, *Le Grand Desert*, 29.

[2] Travels in Tartary, I. c. 3.

them the incessant harsh growl of the camel while loading and unloading, and indeed whenever he is approached by his driver or rider; and barely hint at another, which I will not say 'is more easily imagined than described.' No; as there are heights to which imagination cannot soar, so are there depths to which it cannot descend. I remember one evening and night in Wadee Feiran. No water — thermometer at 110°, air deathly still, and camels *very* near. Oh, for a draught of Lethe! I faint at the recollection. Reader, in hot weather pitch your tent as far from your camels as you dare, and, if there be a breeze, to the windward!"

# CHAPTER VIII.

## USEFUL PRODUCTS OF THE CAMEL.

The milk of the camel is a very favorite drink in all countries where the animal is used. Colonel Chesney, indeed, describes it as poor and slightly saline; but the Arabs, as well as almost all travellers, represent it as highly salubrious and nutritious; and Tavernier vouches for it as a sovereign remedy for the dropsy. It is universally believed to be a corrective of the heating effects of the date, and the Arabs never use that fruit in large quantities without milk. Some of the pastoral tribes possessing large herds, live almost wholly upon it during a great part of the year, and it is frequently given to the mahari and to favorite horses, which are extremely fond of it. It is asserted by the Arabs, that this diet fattens the quarters and shoulders only of the horse, but not the barrel.[1] In a note to a chapter of Daumas, *Les Chevaux du Sahara*,

[1] The camel cannot be fattened, says Burckhardt, after he reaches his sixteenth year.

Abd-el-Kader says: "The inhabitant of the Sahara gives his horse camel's milk, which has the special property of imparting speed to that degree, that, according to what is testified upon responsible and credible testimony, a man, by drinking it exclusively for a sufficient time, acquires such swiftness of foot, that he can successfully contend in the race with the horse. And, in truth, the milk of the camel fortifies the brain and the tendons, and dissipates the fat which relaxes the muscles." The quantity given by the camel, without green food, does not certainly exceed a quart, but the Bactrian, which enjoys a more succulent diet, yields twice that quantity, and it is employed in the Crimea for the same purposes as that of the cow. "Sheikh Hussein had the complaisance to take along with us a milch camel for the use of the ladies of our party, and generally brought the milk-cup to our tents in his own patriarchal hands, with abundance of compliments and salaams. The quantity given by the camel is small, but very rich. Being myself no milksop, I cannot speak of its quality from experience; but the ladies found it both agreeable and refreshing, except that occasionally the highly aromatic pasturage, which, as poets sing, makes fragrant the air of Araby the Blest, gave it a smack of 'pothecary-stuff not altogether so toothsome."

"Although the Bactrian, Turcoman, and Syrian camels are well coated, their Arabian brother has short, coarse, thin hair, except about the chest, shoulders, and hips, where he has a few locks of long, thick wool, and his tail is tufted at the end, and fringed at the sides.[1] I once saw some Bedouins shearing a camel, and the fleece they got reminded me of a similar operation proverbially said to have been performed by a certain personage, who shall be nameless, on his swine; for if there was not 'a great cry,' there was certainly very 'little wool.' The hajéen is close sheared in Egypt, as is the mahari in the Sahara. In the Arabian peninsula, the hair, which Burckhardt says does not exceed two pounds in weight, is generally plucked off by hand. The fleece of the Bactrian averages ten pounds in the Crimea, and that of the same animal and of the cross in Bokhara, and in Cabul, is said, by General Harlan, to be equal in weight to the fleeces of four sheep, while the Turcoman yields not much more than half that quantity. Like the wool of the sheep, it varies exceedingly in fineness and softness, as well as in the length of the staple and in weight. The coarser kinds, some-

1 "The tail is like the two wings of an eagle sewed to the bone with an awl." Arabic poem quoted by Timour, *Méditations Bosphoriques.*

times mixed with goat's hair, are twisted into halter ropes, knit into caps, or woven into webbing, girdles, sackcloth, tent-cloth, and carpets. Among the Tartars, where the wool is finer, cloth of a close texture and great durability is manufactured from it, and Burnes speaks of a 'fine water-proof cloth' of camel's hair, made in Bokhara.[1] In Cabul, cloths are woven from it, says General Harlan, 'approaching in softness the wool of Thibet, and surpassing in silky smoothness and fineness the most delicate flannel.' It is well known that none of the fabrics sold in Western Europe under the name of camel's hair, are made of the wool of this animal. The shawls formerly called camel's hair, but now more generally cashmere, are manufactured from the wool of the Thibet goat, now partially naturalized in France by the joint efforts of Ternaux and Joubert, and other animals of the goat family. And it is a circumstance worth mentioning, that French shawls are woven with Oriental patterns for European consumption, and with European designs for the Eastern market. It appears, however, from Erman, that shawls of an exceedingly fine quality are manufactured in Bokhara, of camel's wool, though they rarely, if ever, find their way

1 The raiment of John the Baptist was of camel's hair. Matthew III. 4.

to the shops of London or Paris. 'Among the wares brought from Bokhara,' (I quote from Erman, Reisen I. 198,) 'are the shawls manufactured there. The Russians affirm, that these precious fabrics are woven from the downy hair of the belly of the dromedary. By means of fine combs, the soft wool is collected from time to time, and spun into yarn as fine as a human hair. These shawls are composed of two strips about eight inches in width, sewed together, and ornamented with figured borders made from the fibrous bark of a plant described by the Russians as a nettle. A white shawl with ornamented borders is often sold for twelve thousand rubles."

The utility of the camel does not cease with his life. His flesh, especially the hump and heart, is a favorite food among all camel-drivers, though most European travellers have found it tough and unsavory. Travellers generally accompany caravans, and seldom reside long among the more stationary tribes in their habitual localities. Upon a march, a camel cannot be slaughtered without transferring his rider or his burden to other beasts, already perhaps overloaded, and he is therefore seldom killed until he falls, or is ready to die, with exhaustion. In this case he is immediately butchered, the Bismillah (in the name of God!) being first pronounced over him. Under such circumstances, his flesh cannot be otherwise than hard and unpalatable. But where the animal is in good case, the flesh appears to be not inferior to that of other domestic quadrupeds. Daumas says, "all the flesh is good, and the hump is the choicest dish a host can offer to guests of distinction." A correspondent in Bessarabia compares it to good beef; and Carbuccia says it is scarcely distinguishable from the flesh of the ox.[1]

The skin is applied to a great variety of uses. "It makes water-skins," says Daumas, "which retain the water in spite of wind and sun, or boots which protect the foot of the traveller against the bite of the viper, and the scorching of the heated sands. Stripped of its hair, soaked, and applied to the frame of a saddle, it fits itself to the shape of the wood, and when dry clings to it like the bark to a tree, without nails or pins." This solidity and density of texture is a point of no small importance in its use

[1] "I have already spoken of the milk, but though I confess to a reasonable degree of enlightened curiosity on the subject of novel aliments, yet I have never carried that laudable passion so far as to partake of barbecued dromedary, or *bifteck de chameau.* I must, therefore, refer my gastronomic readers to the testimony of more diligent and pains-taking inquirers, which, however, is not always very favorable to the savoriness of those outlandish viands." *Journal,* referred to in Preface.

as a material for water-sacks. The goat-skin—of which they are generally made as a matter of convenience, because, when you have stripped off the skin whole, and tied up the apertures, the sack is ready without a stitch—is so porous that the water transpires freely, and soon becomes exhausted, if the sack is exposed to the sun or to drying winds. The skin of the camel is of different degrees of thickness and of strength, according to age and breed; and while some travellers compare it to that of the horse, I am assured that, in the provinces of southern Russia, where it is principally used raw for thongs, straps, and the like, it is not greatly inferior to that of the ox in toughness and durability. In Arabia, it is tanned and dyed yellow with the peels of the pomegranate, or red with a root found in the desert. In Algeria, according to Carbuccia, it is thicker and more valuable than that of the ox.

The tallow, when rendered, is as white as wax, and as a material for candles scarcely inferior to that substance.[1] I do not learn that the bones have been applied to any useful purpose, but from the apparent solidity of the skeletons, which lie scattered along the great desert routes, I have little doubt they would be found useful

1 Ritter XIII. 693. Carbuccia, p. 142.

in the arts. The droppings of the camel are the universal fuel of the desert, and the abundance of this article at the usual places of encampment is one of the reasons why the Arabs are reluctant to stop for the night at any unfrequented station.

# CHAPTER IX.

## DIET, AND POWERS OF ABSTINENCE.

WITH such an organization as is described in Chapter VI. it is obvious that the camel can subsist for a considerable time upon a quantity of food and of water otherwise quite inadequate for the sustenance of so large an animal. It is upon this property that his great value chiefly depends.

By means of the nutriment derived from the absorption of the hump, and the fluid preserved in and perhaps also secreted by the water-sac, he is able to travel several days without any new supplies of either meat or drink. The period of abstinence depends upon the temperature and season, the breed, training, and habits of the particular animal, and the amount of labor demanded of him.

With respect to food, there is no doubt that the camel sometimes endures two, three,[1] and

[1] Carbuccia, p. 15.

even more days of entire privation; but long abstinence from food is seldom necessary, because, although there are well-attested instances of the existence of tracts of desert frequently crossed by caravans, six days' journey in width, and absolutely without a particle of vegetation,[1] yet there are few portions of the Libyan or Arabian deserts where more or less of the shrubs on which the camel feeds do not occur at very much shorter intervals.[2]

[1] Denham and Clapperton, I. c. 3.

[2] Nothing can be more erroneous than the popular impression with regard to the absolute sterility of the desert. As a general rule, it may be stated that no extensive tracts are wholly devoid of winter vegetation except in rainless regions, which are by no means numerous, and which are themselves often interspersed with oases watered by wells, or springs derived from distant and unknown sources. There are few parts of the Libyan desert where water may not be found at moderate depths, and though Shaw, *Travels*, 135, speaks of wells in Wady Reagh one hundred and even two hundred fathoms in depth, yet, in general, water is obtained very near the surface. Wherever there are winter rains, heavy dews in summer, or abundant wells, there is vegetation, arborescent or herbaceous, according to the character of the soil and the supply of moisture; and even in the drought of summer, the twigs, seed-vessels, and withered foliage of the desert plants supply the frugal camel with the necessary nutriment. The Syrian desert, as it is called, between the Hauran and the Euphrates, is in general carpeted with a luxuriant winter vegetation, and though now laid waste by

On the ordinary routes, therefore, the camel is not fed at all, even on long journeys, but is left to snatch his food as he can during the march of the caravan, or gather it more leisurely while it halts. In a journey of seven weeks which I made with these animals in Arabia Petræa, in the months of May and June, but a single camel of the caravan received any food from his driver. This was a fine large animal bred by the Ababdeh Arabs, which was fed at every evening halt with from a pint to a quart of beans. His habit of feeding as he walks is a serious inconvenience to the traveller. At the commencement of the day's march, he is ever on the look-out for the stunted acacias and other prickly plants, which, with occasionally a more succulent herb, constitute almost his sole diet, and he snatches them in passing, giving you an uncomfortable jerk as he turns to seize them, or suddenly stops, at some hazard of throwing you over his stooping shoul-

the wandering Arabs, was once the seat of a dense population. Throughout Arabia Petræa and the greater Arabian Peninsula, the valleys and depressions of the soil, and the more moderate mountain slopes, are thinly dotted with acacias, tamarisks, and numerous arborescent plants. The water-courses of the winter streams, along which lie the usual routes of travel, are marked, when not mere mountain torrents, by belts of reeds and shrubs. Even proper grasses sparingly occur also in small ravines, or on the rocky shelves which retain a little earth and catch the falling moisture.

ders, and, in spite of your most urgent persuasives, browses at his leisure.

Burckhardt,[1] and I think Denham, state, that the African camel is prepared for long journeys by *cramming* him beforehand by actual force, for several days in succession, with three times his usual allowance of dhourra meal,[2] but Father Huc and Timkovski declare that the Bactrian is hardened for the task by several days of previous abstinence, or at least sparing nourishment.

When herbage and browse are altogether wanting, a small quantity of beans, a few handfuls of dates or even date-stones, crushed, or barely softened by soaking in water,[3] a ball or two of dough of barley-meal, dhourra millet, or other grain, or a small supply of some dry vegetable are given each camel daily. According to Edrisi, they are sometimes fed with dried fish. Denham says they are fond of "crunching" dry bones, and Riley even declares that he sometimes saw them fed with charcoal. The favorite food of the camel consists of the leaves, branches,

1 Nubia, 157.

2 Pottinger says that the Belooches thrust a ball of coarse meal and water as large as a child's head into the throat of their dromedaries, and a similar statement is made by Kämpfer. Ritter, *Erdkunde*, XIII. 651.

3 Burckhardt, *Arabia*, 356. Denham and Clapperton, III. c. 3, observe that eating dates after drinking intoxicates camels.

and seed-pods of the acacias and other prickly trees or shrubs, of thistles, and of the saline plants so common in the desert; and almost every vegetable zone is found to furnish some plant specially suited to his nutriment, while, in case of necessity, he scarcely refuses any green thing.[1] His powerful jaws and teeth enable him to grind and masticate branches of the hardest wood as thick as the finger. His palate is lined with a very hard cartilage; and the inside of the lip, the tongue, and the gums are protected by a skin almost equally impenetrable. The lips are, nevertheless, very flexible, and the upper labrum is divided. In feeding on the acacia or other prickly plants, he retracts and partially inverts the lips, grasps the twigs with the tongue and jaws, and thus crops and chews the thorniest shrubs with impunity.

The camels domesticated in Tuscany, which, though degenerated by a residence of centuries

[1] Carbuccia, page 10, says that the camel never touches the "aloe;" but an official report, at page 182 of the same volume, enumerates the "cactus" among the wild vegetables consumed by him. Hammer-Purgstall, p. 17, mentions the coloquintida among the vegetables eaten by the camel. There are two or three species of this bitter plant in the Sinaitic peninsula, in Wady el Araba, and the valleys of Mount Seir, but I have always seen camels, however hungry, refuse them.

in the moist climate and alluvial soil of the lower Arno, are of the Arabian stock, neglect the green and tender cultivated grasses, but devour with avidity the leaves and smaller branches of the oak and the alder, and the hard dry stems of the thorn, the thistle, and the broom. The working camels at the grand duke's farm, near Pisa, are sheltered and fed on hay during the winter, but the rest of the herd remain in the open air, and subsist on twigs and withered shrubs through the cold season.

The Bactrian camel has the same fondness for saline plants as his African congener; but he feeds also upon the leaves, twigs, and bark of deciduous trees, the coarsest grasses, thistles, reeds, rushes, weeds, straw, and, in short, upon such vegetable diet as is rejected by almost every other domestic quadruped.

The statements of travellers differ very considerably with regard to the quantity of solid food required by the camel. My own observation would lead me to think it extremely small. As I have already stated, he is often not fed at all; and in travelling, his only opportunity of gathering his food is between the evening halt and sunset, when he returns to the camp, (for he never feeds in the night,)[1] with such scattering

[1] Burckhardt, *Arabia*, 34. Fraser, *Khorasan*, 379. Tavernier, I. 121.

mouthfuls as he can snatch upon the march. The vegetation of the desert is usually so sparse that the quantity of nutritious food which can be collected after the day's journey is performed must be very inconsiderable; and though upon starting in the morning the animal shows signs of hunger, and much annoys his rider by suddenly stopping or starting aside to crop a tempting thorn, twig or thistle, yet in an hour or two his appetite is satisfied, and he performs the rest of his task without seeming to crave food.[1] I was assured by the keeper of the herd at Pisa, that when fed entirely on hay, the camel consumed little more than half as much as the horse; while, on the other hand, a correspondent in the Crimea informs me that the Bactrian camel requires at least fifty pounds of hay per day in winter, and another in Bessarabia estimates the daily winter supply of hay and straw at seventy pounds.[2] Pottenger states that although the camels of Beloochistan can almost wholly dispense with food for five or six days together, yet they ordinarily receive about fifteen pounds of meal daily, besides grass and shrubs, and he adds the singular fact that the Belooches give these animals

1 Carbuccia says, p. 15 and p. 68, that in good pasturage he consumes enough for the day in two hours.

2 Carbuccia, p. 158, estimates his daily supply of (green) herbage or shrubs at 25 kilos, or about 60 lbs.

considerable quantities of opium and *goor*, a kind of inspissated molasses, with their food. Burckhardt[1] says, that the Berber traders give their camels twelve pounds of dhourra every two or three days, and that, when loaded with burdens of 600 or 700 pounds, they require a daily allowance. The Turkmans, according to the same authority,[2] give their beasts every evening a ball of barley-meal, kneaded with water, and weighing about one pound. The difference in this case is no doubt occasioned by the comparative scarcity and abundance of green fodder, and it may be considered on the whole as established, that the camel thrives and labors with a less proportional supply of nutriment in quantity, and that too of a coarser and cheaper quality, than is required by any other domestic quadruped. The power of the camel to abstain from water is much more frequently and severely tested than his ability to dispense with food. The testimony of travellers, as well as of native observers on this subject varies widely; but their discrepancies can generally be explained by difference of breed, of season, or by the greater or less succulence of the solid food consumed by the animal.

The most extraordinary statements I have

[1] Nubia, 193. [2] Syria, 637.

seen are those of the official reports of the French officers attached to the dromedary corps in Algeria. One of these reports declares that the camels of the corps employed in the expedition of El Aghouat did not drink from February to May, though the weather was very hot;[1] and General Carbuccia, the commander of the corps, states that the Algerine camel never drinks during the last two months of autumn, and the entire winter and spring. He adds,[2] "at the beginning of summer, he drinks, and then abstains fifteen days. After having drunk again, he goes fourteen days without water, then thirteen, then twelve, &c., and finally seven days, diminishing gradually his periods of abstinence by a day. After this, he drinks every seven days, and not oftener, whatever may be the heat, or the fatigues of the journey." Unfortunately for the credit of this remarkable story, Carbuccia[3] himself, p. 159, contradicts it, by stating that when the camel feeds on the guettaf, a saline shrub, he drinks every day from the 15th of June to the end of winter. Burnes says that in Bokhara he goes two or three days without water, but becomes feeble, and finally dies on the fourth day, or sooner if the weather is hot.

1 'Même par les plus fortes chaleurs.' Carbuccia, p. 204.

2 Du Dromadaire, p. 15.

3 Ib. 159.

Burckhardt[1] states that the camel of Asia Minor, which seldom drinks in winter, requires water every other day in summer, and if longer deprived of it frequently dies on the third. The Nedjd camel will often die if not watered by the evening of the fourth day, and he declares that in Arabia the utmost limit of abstinence in summer is four, or possibly in some cases five days, though the animal shows signs of great distress after the third. The camel of Nubia and the Sahara has much greater powers of endurance in this respect. Denham and Clapperton, I. c. 3, mention a case of eight days' entire privation of water, with *dry* food. Burckhardt[2] records an instance of like abstinence, of the same duration, in the month of August, and in his Notes on the Bedouins, 259, he ascribes to the camels of Darfur the power of dispensing with water for nine or ten days, even when on the march. The Tibboos and other tribes, who constantly traverse the Sahara, are very confidently affirmed to possess camels which can support a privation of fifteen days without serious inconvenience; but this belief rests on native authority, and I can find no European traveller who testifies upon personal observation to a longer abstinence, *in the dry*

[1] Bedouins, 258. [2] Nubia, 186.

*season*, than in the cases cited from Burckhardt and Denham and Clapperton. I have myself witnessed in Arabia Petræa an instance of complete privation for four days, in very hot weather and with dry fodder, but I have always observed that in the summer, the camel, like the Bedouin, drinks as often as he has the opportunity. In most countries where the animal is used, it is said he can dispense with drinking twice as long as the horse under the same circumstances; and this I doubt not is a very near general approximation to the truth. These facts, however wonderful, are by no means so extraordinary or incredible as they may at first sight appear. The animals of the deer and antelope tribes which inhabit the Sahara often pass many weeks together in the heat of summer, in the most parched districts of the great Libyan Desert, without possibility of access to any known supply of water, and they probably possess powers of abstinence at least equal if not superior to those of the camel. The domestic ox, when supplied with abundance of green fodder, seldom inclines to drink. Persons familiar with sheep husbandry know that in rich pastures that animal thrives very well for many weeks in the hottest summers, without any water but that which falls in the shape of dew. If I mistake not, Captain Stansbury's mules travelled two whole days along the margin of Salt Lake without food or water, and Abd-el-Kader, in a letter cited in Daumas,[1] says, " our horses went a day or two without drinking, and on one occasion they found no water for three days." In fact, the Arab horse is seldom allowed to drink oftener than once in twenty-four hours.

The quantity of water taken by the camel after long privation is very great, and one would hardly believe that the fluid could be driven by a forcing-pump through so long, narrow, and crooked a channel as this animal's gullet, so rapidly as he swallows it. Carbuccia, p. 15, says he drinks from thirty to forty litres. Burckhardt[2] estimates his usual quantity at from fifty to one hundred pounds. I have seen a camel empty at a draught three goat-skins, holding not less than seven gallons each. Riley speaks of even much larger quantities, and Russell says that after long thirst they sometimes drink so greedily that it proves suddenly fatal to them.

He smells, or by some other perception detects, water at the distance of a mile or more. The whole caravan, disdaining all control, rushes confusedly to the pool, to the great injury of the luggage, and the imminent peril of the knees and ankles of the rider, which he can secure from bruising only by drawing them up under him,

[1] Les Chevaux du Sahara, 405. [2] Nubia, 79.

and sitting *à la Turque*, on a very wavering and unstable foundation.

It is not the mere power of abstinence alone that so eminently fits the camel for traversing the steppe and the desert. His preference for the brackish and even saline waters which almost exclusively occur in those regions, and which are often so highly impregnated with mineral substances as to be rejected by most other quadrupeds, is a property almost as valuable. Russell even states that he chooses salt water rather than fresh, and Burckhardt[1] affirms that both camels and horses drink the sea-water left by the ebb of the tide in the wadys communicating with the Red Sea. I do not think, however, that this is the common habit of the animal, for I do not find it mentioned by other writers, and I have seen them, when parched with thirst, rush to the sea, wade into it, and turn from it, with evident disappointment on finding it salt.

The elder Pliny and some modern writers say that the camel purposely makes the water turbid before drinking, as has been alleged of the horse, by stirring the mud at the bottom with the foot; but as neither of these quadrupeds can usually reach the surface of a pool or river without wading into it, it is much more probable that the disturbance of the fluid is an unintentional one.

[1] Syria, 661.

## CHAPTER X.

### TRAINING AND TREATMENT.

THE breaking in of the camel commences when he is very young, and the *manège* of the ordinary animal is very simple and soon completed. The high-bred dromedary, however, requires a careful training, which, as Daumas says, occupies more than an entire year of the time of his groom. Tavernier states, that the new-born foal is made to lie down, folding his legs under him, and covered with a cloth, the edges of which are loaded with stones to confine him in this posture. He is thus kept fifteen or twenty days, and in the mean time sparingly fed with milk. The object of this treatment is said to be to accustom him to lie upon his belly rather than his side, and to enure him to thirst. It is quite certain that young camels intended for burden are not usually subjected to such a regimen, and notwithstanding Tavernier's general accuracy, it may be doubted whether the foal requires any teaching to adopt the mode of lying down which his physical structure prescribes. The fact, nevertheless, that such a training was pursued elsewhere than in the countries visited by Tavernier, appears from the account given by Brue, a Frenchman, who travelled in Senegal towards the close of the seventeenth century, and who describes the process in much the same words. At present, however, it is believed that the only education generally bestowed upon the ordinary animal is simply to habituate him gradually to the halter and the pack-saddle, and to teach him to lie down and rise at the word of command. Nature and the imitation of his fellows do the rest. I quote at length, from Daumas,[1] his description of the training of the mahari of the Sahara.

"As soon as the foal is dropped, he is swaddled with a broad band to compress his intestines and prevent the belly from acquiring too great a volume. The bandages are removed in eight days. The young mahari is an inmate of the tent, a playfellow of the children, and habit and gratitude attach him to the family, whom he feels to be his friends. In the spring he is sheared, and for a year he sucks when he pleases, and follows his dam at will. He is not yet troubled with lessons, and is as free as if in a wild state. When the time for weaning arrives, one of his nostrils is pierced with a sharp stick,

[1] *Mœurs et Coutumes de l'Algérie.*

which is left remaining in the wound,[1] and when he attempts to suck, it pricks the udder of the dam, which repulses him with kicks, and he soon abandons the teat for the fresh grass of the season. He is again sheared in the spring, and at the close of the second year, his education commences. For the first lesson, they put upon him a halter, the rein of which is made to shackle one of his legs, and he is kept motionless, at first by gestures and the voice, and then by the voice alone. The halter is now loosened from his leg, but replaced if he takes a step. He now begins to understand what is wanted, and this lesson is repeated until he will stand a whole day with his halter dragging, where his master has placed him. An iron ring is now passed through the right nostril and permanently riveted. To this is attached a rein of camel's-hair rope, carried from right to left, and connecting on the shoulder with the rein of the halter, which passes up on the other side. He is next accustomed to the

[1] This would seem almost incredible, were it not confirmed by the authority of Burckhardt. "The young camel is weaned at the beginning of his second year. He is prevented from sucking by driving a sharp wooden pin, four inches long, through the palate and nostrils. The Turcomans tie a sharp stick across the nostrils instead. Before weaning, the foal is prevented from sucking too often by tying up the udder in a camel's-hair bag, or a wooden bowl." *Bedouins*, 111.

*rahkala*, or dromedary saddle. This is of a concave form, with a broad, high back, and elevated pommel, and the rider sits as in a bowl, crossing his legs over the neck of his dromedary, and secured on all sides by the support of the saddle. The least pull of the rein upon the nose-ring is so painful to the animal, that he always, passively, moves to the right or left, advances, or steps backward, at the will of his rider.

"To teach him to kneel when the rider cries *sh, sh, sh!* an attendant strikes his knees at the moment the cry is uttered, and until he kneels at the word. His pace is quickened by the whip accompanied with a shrill ejaculation. He is taught to stop suddenly at whatever rate of speed, if his rider falls or leaps from the saddle, and to describe a small circle around a lance which his master plants in the ground, and resume the gallop as soon as he plucks it up.[1] His training is now complete. He is no longer a colt, but a mahari."

Although this account is derived from the best sources, it must not be imagined that the common dromedary receives a training by any means so finished, and it is only upon the more

[1] "The Bedja camel follows the lance when thrown, that his master may recover it, and if it falls to the ground, he stoops with his hind quarters to allow him to pick it up." Makrizi, as quoted by Burckhardt, *Nubia*, 458.

promising foals, or the high-blooded breeds, that these extraordinary pains are bestowed.

The young camel is able to stand and walk at his birth. If he is dropped upon a march, an event by no means uncommon, he is generally carried for a day in the arms of a slave on foot, or on the back of the dam, after which he is left to follow her as he can, and he usually manages to keep up with the caravan. "A young lady of my party," says a writer often quoted, "rode several days with a new-born foal tied to the tail of her dromedary, and the brisky juvenile appeared to have little difficulty in keeping pace with his mamma, although occasionally, in the latter part of the day's journey, his tow-line, which in the morning had a good deal of slack, would get hauled rather taut."

The Bedouin regards the foaling of a camel with much the same feelings as Sterne's Obadiah greeted the advent of his calf. "Lo! another child is born to us," cries he, upon the arrival of the youthful stranger, and he receives him with almost as much interest and affection as he bestows on the new-born heir of his tent, and of the flocks, which constitute the only wealth of the nomade tribes. The camel is almost uniformly treated with much gentleness by the wandering Arabs, though the Egyptians and other nations who are less dependent upon them, as well as the Bedouins who border upon the valley of the Nile, often deal very harshly with them. Speaking of the latter people, St. John, in his narrative of his visit to the oasis of Siwah, says: "The Bedouin has no affection for his camel. He starves him on principle, to accustom him to it, and maltreats and neglects him." Indeed, the expression of anxiety and often terror, which the camel assumes upon being approached, seems to indicate an expectation of ill-treatment, and a consciousness of the inability to resist or resent it; but there is certainly little in his ordinary treatment by the desert tribes to warrant his timid apprehensions.

The camel displays no inconsiderable sagacity. He detects springs in localities where they have not before been known to exist, and tradition affirms that even the holy fountain Zemzem was not revealed to man, but discovered by a stray camel. Upon frequented routes, the drivers leave them to their own guidance, sleeping the while, and if by any chance the track is lost, the whole troop is soon in a state of alarm and confusion. It is even said that when the caravan is led astray by the ignorance of the guides, the camels are soon aware of it and become quite ungovernable with terror.

It is a popular belief that the camel has a musical ear, and it is said that the drivers in some countries carry flutes to cheer and enliven their animals when weary with the march. In my narrow experience, I have witnessed no such practice, but the Arabs often commence towards the close of the day's journey, a wild chant in the minor key[1] which, as they allege, perceptibly enlivens and inspirits the camel, but I cannot say that I have seen any very obvious effects from it.

Hammer-Purgstall, p. 69, observes that "the drivers accomplish more by the chant than by blows," and that the Arabs have words to designate the particular effect of song on the music-loving camel. "The camel," says he, p. 95, "loves singing better than mere shouting, and marches more cheerfully to its tones. The chanting driver, no longer urging his beast by blows or words, does not follow the camel, but walks before him. Camels particularly fond of singing have special names, and there are appellations appropriated to musical drivers; it even appears that caravans are accompanied by

1 The music of the Arabs is hardly reducible to our system of notation. The musical reader will find a very curious article on this subject in one of the early volumes of the transactions of the American Oriental Society. It is an Essay on Arab music by Mr. Meshaka, a highly cultivated Christian Arab of Deir el Hamer in Syria, with notes and additions by Prof. Salisbury of Yale College.

camel-singers when the drivers cannot chant.' Hammer-Purgstall, it will be observed, does not mention *instrumental* music as employed for this purpose.

By long familiarity and close observation, the Arab acquires a wonderfully minute acquaintance, not only with the general characteristics of the camel, but with the physical peculiarities which distinguish his particular beasts. Thus Burckhardt says they readily trace an estray by his track, and every wanderer in the desert sees daily proofs of a power which they possess in common with other tribes, whose life depends on a thorough knowledge of particulars, that among civilized nations are regarded as unimportant. That most admirable traveller, Layard, whose knowledge of the character and habits of the Arabs and other races that compose the population of the Turkish empire is unrivalled, affirms that the Bedouin, from marks left by the camel, will tell whether he was loaded or unloaded, full or hungry, fatigued or fresh, the time of his passing, whether the rider was an inhabitant of the desert or the town, a friend or a foe, and sometimes even his tribe. "My deloul," adds, he "has even been led by my guide, that those who might cross our path might not detect that it was ridden by one not thoroughly accustomed to the management of the animal."

With a trivial exception, to be noticed hereafter, the camel is never housed or sheltered in all the wide range of climates through which he is diffused. Tavernier says he is sometimes gently beaten with a small rod by way of curry-comb, but in general he receives no dressing, washing, or care whatever, except the administration of medicaments in disease. That more attention on the part of his drivers would be well repaid, there can be little doubt; but among civilized nations, there would be some danger of error upon the other side, especially in abridging him of that liberty of roving, which seems to be a necessary condition of his existence.

# CHAPTER XI.

## BURDEN AND FURNITURE.

The camel, with his slender and shrunken limbs, his light quarters, and his shambling gait, seems little adapted to the performance of any labor requiring either speed or strength; but his powers of endurance enable him to accomplish a long journey in a shorter space than even the horse; and he bears a burden greatly disproportioned to his own weight. The camel of the great Arabian Peninsula, though remarkable for his speed, is less powerful than the Bactrian, the Turcoman, the Syrian, or the Egyptian animal. In Arabia Petræa, his load does not ordinarily exceed three or four hundred pounds. Brown estimates the burdens of the camels of Soudan at the same weight; and Burckhardt that of the Nubian camel at four or five hundred pounds. In India, according to Forbes,[1] his proper burden is five hundred pounds, though some powerful animals may carry from

[1] Oriental Memoirs, II. 69.

six hundred to seven hundred. Fraser states his load in Khorasan at from four hundred and fifty to seven hundred pounds. Colonel Chesney found the loads of a caravan of several hundred camels, in the Syrian desert, to average five hundred and fifty pounds, though he elsewhere states their common burden to be six hundred.

In Algeria, he carries two or three hundred kilogrammes, (450 to 675 pounds,) but at Cairo, according to Burckhardt, fifteen hundred pounds for a distance of three miles, and one thousand from Cairo to Suez, which is eighty-four miles. In Cabul, according to General Harlan,[1] the burden of the Arabian camel is, upon the plains, four hundred pounds; that of the cross between the Bactrian and Arabian, under similar circumstances, six hundred, and over mountainous roads four hundred pounds. In European Turkey, the one-humped camel is said to carry from four to five hundred pounds; and Burnes estimates the load of the same animal in Bokhara at five hundred pounds. The burden of the Turcoman camel, according to Burckhardt, is eight hundred pounds; Forbes rates it from seven hundred to one thousand, Fraser one hundred pounds higher, and Tavernier at one thousand; and, for short distances, even fifteen

[1] U. S. Pat. Rep. 1853, Agric. 61.

hundred. Timkovski states the burden of the Bactrian of Northern Tartary at from four hundred and twenty to four hundred and eighty pounds; Erman,[1] at about six hundred pounds. Burnes estimates that of the same animal in Bokhara at six hundred and fifty pounds, and Bergmann, among the Calmucks, at eight hundred. I was told by one of the keepers of the Grand Duke's camels, at his farm near Pisa, that these animals would carry their own weight, which he estimated at twelve or thirteen hundred pounds, but I thought the weight of the burden and probably that of the camel exaggerated.

Numerous other authorities might be cited, but the result would not be essentially varied. The pound used by these different writers is, probably, not always the same weight, and this circumstance may explain, to some extent, the difference in their estimates. Almost all authors agree in saying that the northern breeds are much stronger than the southern; but the difference in this respect does not appear to be important, though there is little doubt that, in northern climates, at least, the cross is to be preferred, as a beast of burden, to either of the pure species. The ability of the camel to rise under his load is a common measure of the bur-

[1] Reisen I. 410.

den he can carry; but it would hardly be a safe test in a mountainous country, or on ground otherwise unfavorable. We shall probably not err widely in assuming from five to seven hundred pounds as a general average of the camel's burden, according to the weight of the animal, the smoothness or ruggedness of the route, and the distance to be travelled; and with the smallest of these loads good animals would easily surmount any mountain passes practicable to other beasts of burden. The weight of the pack-saddle, which is considerable, is excluded in these estimates. Although the camel of both species may be said to be most generally used as a beast of burden, yet the Arabian sometimes, and the Bactrian often, are employed for draught. Athenæus,[1] mentions six double spans of camels as figuring in a ceremonial procession of one of the Ptolemies, at Alexandria. Seetzen[2] saw a single camel harnessed to the plough, near Hebron, drawing by the shoulder, and Minutoli represents the animal as employed for the same purpose in Egypt, as, according to Chesney and Colonel Tod, he is also in Afghanistan and Sinde. I have seen them drawing large stones upon wheels in Egypt, and Mehemet Ali and others have used them for transporting heavy ordnance. These were all of the

[1] L. v. c. 32. [2] Reisen III. 31.

one-humped species. Although the Calmucks, and other half-civilized and savage tribes in the remote territories of Russia, and in Independent Tartary, employ the Bactrian only for the saddle and for burdens, yet Timkovski saw a carriage drawn by this animal in the desert of Gobi, and he is used in Bessarabia for riding, for the plough, and for draught; in the Crimea for draught alone, being seldom ridden in the latter province. Demidoff describes the wagons (madjars) drawn by these animals as clumsy four-wheeled vehicles of wood, "without a particle of iron," and speaks with admiration of the strength and docility displayed by the camels. They are simply yoked to the pole in the same manner as oxen are with us, and have no other gearing. I have elsewhere stated that a pair of them will make long journeys with a load of three thousand or four thousand pounds.

In whatever mode the camel is employed, his harness and furniture are very simple, and as the dromedary is not often a *monture de luxe*, he is, even when ridden by persons of consideration, seldom decked with trappings so showy as those of a favorite horse. The camel is sometimes guided by a plain halter,[1] sometimes the septum,

1 "The halter is of the simplest form, handsomely twisted of goat's and camel's hair, sometimes tastefully decorated

or one of the alæ of the nose is pierced, an iron ring inserted, and a cord attached to this to serve as a bridle. The French, in their military service, have found it convenient to use both the halter and this rude bridle in conjunction. Instead of the ring, Meyer found that, in Siberia, the hair-cord of the halter was sometimes passed through the septum, and Burckhardt observes that, in Nubia, the males, when unruly, are controlled in the same way, though, in Arabia, the nose is seldom pierced. In Northern Tartary, according to Erman,[1] and Father Huc, a semicircular bone or piece of wood is passed through the septum of the nose, and the reins of the halter, or rather bridle, are attached to the ends, which project a couple of inches on each

with cowries, fringes, and other ornaments, and furnished with a loop for throwing over the saddle-peg, or otherwise securing it. In racing, it is attached to a ring in the nostrils, but generally passes round the nose like a common stable-halter, and the use of the bit is quite unknown. If you are a green hand, an Arab leads your dromedary for a day's journey or so, and then intrusts you with the halter; which, as soon as you feel at home on your beast, you throw over the pummel, unless you are one of those fidgetty, ill-bred persons, who don't know what to do with their hands, when they are not quill-driving or knitting; in which case, sir or madam, you may hold the halter, and occupy your digits in playing with the tassel at the end of it."

*The Desert, Am. Whig Review, ubi supra.*

[1] Reisen, II. 135.

side, and are somewhat larger than the middle of the bone. The bit is nowhere used, nor am I aware that it has ever been even tried. It would seriously interfere with the animal's habit of feeding as he walks, but the mahari is seldom allowed to do this, and it might, perhaps, answer for that variety. There does not, indeed, appear to be any urgent necessity for its introduction, nor is there, on the other hand, any very obvious objection to its use. Perhaps a leather ring around the nose, like that which is often used at Naples and elsewhere in southern Italy instead of a bit, and armed with blunt points within, in something the same way, might be an improvement on the common camel-halter.

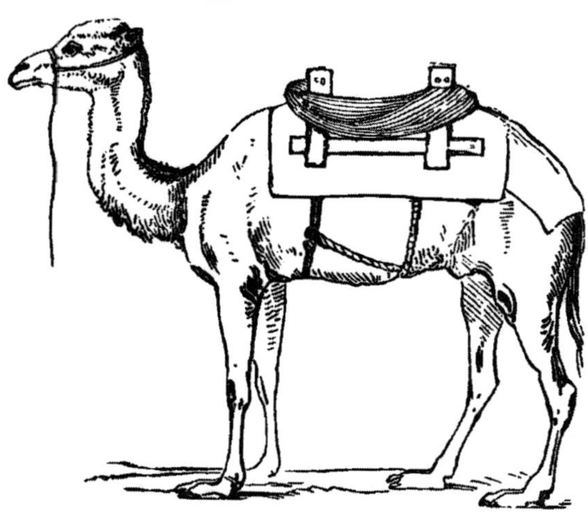

ARABIAN CAMEL: PACK-SADDLE.

The pack-saddle, whether for riding or for burden, is made by stuffing a bag seven or eight feet long with straw or grass, doubling it and sewing the ends together. This forms an oblong ring, which is furnished with a rope crupper and placed upon the back so as to inclose the hump. Upon this cushion rests a frame consisting of two pairs of flat sticks meeting at top like a chevron or pair of rafters, and connected at bottom by a couple of sticks two or three feet long, secured to the others by thongs. The pad soon fits itself to the shape of the back and sides, and the frame nestles into the pad, while the hump rising in the centre of the whole apparatus keeps everything in place, so that no girth, or at most a loose rope, is needed to confine the saddle. The load stowed in sacks, or better still in rope nettings, is balanced across the saddle, and the water-skins are suspended beneath.

The pack saddle of the Bactrian must of course be modified to suit the different configuration of the back, but it is substantially like that of the Arabian animal. The double hump creates some inconvenience in arranging the pad, and an impression that the humps are too sensitive to allow of loading the backs extensively prevails. It is for these reasons, no doubt, that the Bactrian is little used for burdens in Cabul or the Russian provinces, on the Black Sea, but the objections have not elsewhere been found formidable enough to interfere seriously with the usefulness of the animal. Erman says expressly that he saw them at Kiachta, with bales on both sides of their pack-saddles.

"This," says a writer before quoted; "is the entire harness of the burden camel when, as is usual in the desert, he is left at liberty. Elsewhere he is provided with a simple halter, and tied head to tail, in strings, properly of seven animals, the hindermost wearing a bell, in order that the driver who rides the file leader, (or perhaps a donkey, as being a beast of softer pace and easier guidance,) may be advertised of any solution of continuity in the chain by the fainter sound of the accustomed ding-dong."[1]

As the camel lies down to receive and discharge his burden, he is very quickly and conve-

1 Tavernier, *Voyages*, I. 121, saw camels in divisions of seven connected with each other by a rope attached to the pack-saddle, and tied to the nose-ring of the camel following by a small cord made purposely weak, so that if one fell, the cord might break without pulling down another, or tearing his nose. Burckhardt, *Nubia*, 388, says, that in Nubia and the Hedjar, the camels are made to march in *file*, because if the load of one of them requires arranging he can be led out of the file, and reloaded before the last of the train has passed, whereas, when they travel in *line*, the whole caravan must halt if one is obliged to stop. In Egypt, and in the Syrian desert, the caravans march in line, and a caravan of 2,000 show a front of a mile. There is evidently some mistake in this. A camel, with a pack-saddle, occupies hardly less than six feet of front, and allowing nothing for intervals, a caravan of 2,000 would extend more than two miles. In fact they could not be made to advance in a smaller space than four miles at the least.

niently loaded and unloaded; the latter operation generally consisting simply in loosing a knot of the cord by which the packages are slung across the saddle, and the camel then immediately rises and goes in search of pasture. On returning to the camp at evening he lies down between the packages; and if these consist of merchandise or other articles not requiring to be opened at night, the driver has only to knot the cord again, and the animal is ready for the march.[1] The pack-saddle is very rarely removed; and as the camel very seldom stretches himself on his side or attempts to roll, the saddle is never lost.[2]

The gear of the dromedary is somewhat lighter, but of the same fashion. The wooden frame is more neatly made, the uprights being curved outwards and uniting at top in two conical pommels, one before and one behind, six or eight

[1] Tavernier, I. 130. Forbes says, that two men will load or unload twenty-five camels in half an hour.

[2] Carbuccia says, p. 5, that the camel rolls like other quadrupeds, but p. 131, he observes that one of the cords which confine the pack-saddle is merely loosened at night, and the animal turned out to feed. The removal of the pack-saddle at night would much expose the animal to chills, and Daumas refers to the danger of removing even the loading before the animal is cooled. The pack-saddle is certainly not ordinarily removed at night, and I have never seen a camel roll, or, so far as I remember, lie upon its side.

inches high, and perhaps two in diameter at the base, covered with figured brass plate or otherwise decorated, and terminating in a knob, after the manner of the finial of a gothic pediment. Over the saddle is thrown a large pair of saddle-bags of striped goat's-hair cloth, ornamented with fringes and cowrie shells, and upon this are laid blankets, cushions, and carpets, and perhaps a gay housing over all. The rider is perched at the summit of this pyramid, directly over or perhaps a little in advance of the hump; and his stirrups, if he uses them, his *zemzemeek* or leather water-bottle, his gun, a smaller pair of saddle-bags or a carpet-bag, or any other convenience he may choose, (for there is room for all,) are hung to the pommels. In riding the mahari, however, the Tuaricks, and other wild tribes, sit on, or rather in, a small saddle much in the form of a bowl, placed in front of the hump, upon the withers, and secured by girths. They hold a tight rein, and steady themselves by crossing their ankles on the camel's neck. The saddle used for the dromedary in Nubia, according to Burckhardt, much resembles that of the horse. When riding without a saddle, the Bedouin sits behind the hump, and holds by the long hair which decorates that appendage. This extreme simplicity and economy of harness has, with trifling modifications, been carried into the military service by the French in Algeria, and wherever else the camel has been employed in war, and is found to answer all purposes as completely as the costly furniture with which we supply our cavalry. Every soldier may be his own saddler, and he requires no material but bagging, straw or grass, a little cordage, and a few small sticks, which may be found wherever there is any arborescent vegetation, to extemporize at an hour's warning the complete equipage of his beast.

Invalids, and luxurious persons, require more artificial arrangements for travelling on the camel. "Ladies, both paynim and Christian, do generally *bestride* the dromedary, after the ensample of the lords of the creation, but when the delicacy, the health, or the dignity of dame or seignior forbid this, Arab ingenuity hath contrived other means of transportation. The simplest is the *shibreeyeh*, a sort of platform composed of mattresses, carpets, and cushions, resting on a pair of luggage chests, or other scaffolding secured to the pack-saddle, and with or without an awning. This may be long enough to allow the traveller to sit or lie at will. The next is the *moosultah*, which, in its rudest form, consists of a couple of frames much resembling old-fashioned high-backed chairs, except that they are considerably larger, and have the seat, or rather flooring, at the bottom of the legs.

These frames are suspended uprightly across the pack-saddle, the travellers squat uncomfortably within them, and an awning supported partly by the high backs is thrown over them. You will sometimes meet a whole harem, (not indeed so large as Sultan Solomon's,) stowed away in a moosultah; and I once saw a mother and three pickaninnies of 'assorted sizes' riding in one of these contrivances. There is another much less objectionable form of this apparatus, which is not unfrequently used by ladies of rank or persons in ill health. It was called a *mahafa* by our dragoman and Arabs, though Lane ignores both the name and the thing, which is remarkable, considering that it is not uncommon in Egypt. The mahafa consists of a pair of boxes, or rather frames, some five feet long, two or more wide, and about two deep, with posts at the *outer* corners, and a wooden bottom. These frames, like those of the moosultah, are hung across the pack-saddle, and a large and usually showy awning is supported over all by the posts at the corners and another resting on the pack-saddle in the centre, besides which it has side curtains, or when used by Mussulman women, perhaps lattices. In order to balance the mahafa, it must carry two persons, or, if there be but one, an equivalent weight as a counterpoise on the other side. The weight of the mahafa is considerable, and with the necessary mattresses and cushions, and two persons, it makes a heavy load for an Arabian camel, and is of course quite out of the question for a proper dromedary. It is at best an uncomfortable conveyance, but invalids can hardly travel otherwise, and their ease may be very much promoted by substituting for the wooden bottom a frame with a stout tight sacking. Last and most luxurious of all, is the *takhtirawan*, or camel-litter, which, from its great length, can only be used on routes of convenient width, and free from steep grades and sharp corners, and is therefore unsuited to ordinary desert travel. The takhtirawan has a general resemblance to a coach-body resting on two very long shafts, and is borne by two camels, walking between the shafts as in thills, one before and one behind. It is generally intended for two persons, but Pietro della Valle says that the *comoda e galante* takhtirawan, which he had made at Ispahan for the conveyance of the fair and courageous Maani and her damsels, allowed convenient space for four to sit, or three to lie. According to Lane, 'the head of the hinder camel is painfully bent down under the vehicle.'[1] Della Valle does not men-

[1] Burckhardt, *Arabia*, 263, speaks of the takhtirawan as used by Pachas and other great people, and he mentions seeing the heads of the camels that bore one of these vehicles " bent down *by fatigue*," but does not say that they were kept down by the form of the takhtirawan.

tion this circumstance, and I should imagine that, by giving the shafts a proper length, the necessity of it might be avoided."

The account given in the above extract corresponds with the descriptions of most travellers, except in the nomenclature. The apparatus styled *moosultah* in the extract is called by Burckhardt *shekdof*, by Seetzen *schäckadif*, and Tavernier, Lyon, and Burnes apply the name of *cajava* or *kajawah* to the *mahafa*, for which latter term I find no authority. Burnes complains, that in travelling in a *kajawah*, he at first suffered from sea-sickness, but he was able to read and take notes, which is hardly practicable in any other mode of camel-riding. A more extraordinary vehicle than any of the foregoing is described and figured by Layard. This is a light framework of cane, sixteen or twenty feet long, covered with parchment and ornamented, as are also the body and neck of the camel which bears it, with tassels and fringes of worsted of every hue, and strings of glass beads and shells. The frame is balanced athwart the pack-saddle, and in a sort of pavilion in the centre sits the high-born lady, its occupant, the arms of the frame extending on both sides like the wings of a butterfly, and not less gaudy and variegated. The motion is described as swaying and uncomfortable. Of course, none of these contrivances admit of rapid motion, and they are only suited for feeble persons and comparatively short and slow journeys.

## CHAPTER XII.

### SPEED AND GAIT.

THE rate of travel of the burden camel is exceedingly uniform, and it varies little in the different species and breeds of the animal. It has been made a matter of careful study by many travellers, with a view to its employment in geography, as a measure of distance. Burnes observed, that a file of twenty-two camels occupied a distance of ninety-four yards, and that they passed over this space in one minute and a half, or ninety seconds, which gives a speed of two miles and about three hundred yards per hour. Upon a sandy soil, he found a diminution of the rate, for which he allows one hundred yards per hour, and like all other travellers, he remarked that the step was naturally quicker in the night or early morning, than in the heat of the day, or at the close of a fatiguing march. Over a smooth and level surface, I have found his ordinary length of step to be six feet, and the number of steps of each foot to be thirty-seven to the minute. This gives a speed of two miles and fifty-two hundredths to the hour, under the most favorable circumstances.[1] Upon rougher ground, it is of course proportionately retarded. Robinson has investigated this subject with his usual care, and upon an examination of the best authorities, adopts, as the result for the caravan of loaded camels, an average speed of two and one third miles per hour. The speed is of course greatly modified by the nature of the ground, and other contingencies, but all irregularities of

[1] Carbuccia, p. 21, says, "The *walk* of the camel on level ground is eighty-five steps of $1^{m.}$ 25 to the minute." This would give a speed of four miles the hour, which is much beyond the truth, and it will be observed, that the number of steps to the minute is nearly twice that stated by Col. Chesney, although the length of step is much less. (See *post* in this chapter.) In p. 132, he tells us that the camel marches *more slowly* than the infantry, but as he does not halt, he arrives earlier at the bivouac. A report by Capt. Aubac of the French army, Carbuccia, p. 200, states, that on a march of 30,000 mètres, the camels gained four hours and a quarter upon the infantry, and upon a march of 28,000 mètres, they gained three hours. On these occasions, they carried burdens of nearly three hundred pounds, a fagot of wood and a goat-skin of water, besides a rider, weighing in all certainly five hundred pounds. During a part of the march they trotted and even galloped, and Capt. Aubac adds, that the camel if pressed, will gain upon the infantry fifteen minutes the hour. Carbuccia can be reconciled neither with this report nor with himself. His facts and his opinions must always be received with caution, and I have seldom quoted him, except where he is supported by other authority.

this sort are usually compensated in long journeys, and I have no doubt that Robinson's estimate is as near an approximation to the truth as the nature of the case admits.

The length of the caravan day's journey, when there is no special motive for haste, is regulated by the distance between wells and pasture-grounds; but it is seldom less than ten, and more frequently twelve or fourteen hours, and in most countries the entire day's journey is performed without a halt. Burnes says, the camel of Bokhara travels fourteen successive hours, or about thirty miles per day, and that on one occasion he accomplished seventy miles with a caravan in forty-four hours, stops included. Burckhardt travelled at the rate of ten hours per day, for thirty-five days together, resting only a single day. Lyon [1] says the camels of the Sahara march without a halt from sixteen to twenty hours, and many other travellers confirm these accounts, all of which refer to the *camelus dromedarius*, or one-humped camel.

But this falls short of the ordinary performances of the Bactrian of the Crimea and independent Tartary. Bergmann states the ordinary day's journey of this variety at forty miles, and without burden, at from fifty to sixty-five miles. Correspondents of my own, who have had long

[1] Travels in Africa, 91.

and excellent facilities for observation in Bessarabia and the Crimea, where the Bactrian is used principally for draught with wheel carriages, agree in saying that upon a good dry road, a pair of these animals will draw a load of from three thousand to four thousand pounds a distance of fifty miles without eating, drinking, or halting. It would certainly be entirely safe to average the day's journey of both species at ten hours, or twenty-three miles per day, and there is very little doubt that, with due care and attention, thirty miles per day can be averaged by caravans for any desirable length of time. This is the estimate for animals with full burdens, and left to their natural gait, but in case of emergency, and with lighter loads, both the rate of travel and the length of the day's march may in all probability be much increased, at least for moderate distances. There can be no doubt, therefore, that on soils and in climates adapted to his organization, the camel, as a beast of draught or burden, is decidedly superior to the horse, the ox, or any other domestic animal.

The value of the camel as a beast of the saddle for *general* use, is more questionable, but he may be advantageously employed for personal transportation under many conditions, and in many localities where neither the horse nor the mule can be used. Many of the Arab accounts of the fleetness of the mahari are no doubt fables, and one may well question whether Jackson's story of the dromedary that bore his master on an errand of love from Morocco to Mogador and back, a distance of two hundred miles, in a single day, is not exaggerated. But the numerous well-authenticated evidences of this animal's great speed and power of endurance, leave no doubt that in the union of these two qualities he far surpasses the horse, as well as all other domestic quadrupeds.

Mehemet Ali, when hastening to his capital to accomplish the destruction of the Mamelukes, rode without changing his camel, from Suez to Cairo, a distance of eighty-four miles, in twelve hours. A French officer in the service of the Pacha, repeated the same feat in thirteen hours, and two gentlemen of my acquaintance have performed it in less than seventeen. Laborde travelled the distance in the same time, and afterwards rode the same dromedary from a point opposite Cairo to Alexandria, a distance of about one hundred and fifty miles, in thirty-four hours. But the most extraordinary well-authenticated performance of the dromedary is that recorded by the accurate Burckhardt in his Travels.[1] The owner of a fine dromedary laid a wager that he would ride the animal from Esneh to Keneh, and back, a distance of one hundred

[1] Nubia, 262.

and twenty-five miles, between sun and sun. He accomplished one hundred and fifteen miles, occupying twenty minutes in crossing and recrossing the Nile by ferry in eleven hours, and then gave up the wager. Burckhardt thinks this dromedary would have travelled one hundred and eighty or two hundred miles in twenty-four hours without serious injury. The valuable paper extracted from the notes of General Harlan, and printed in the U. S. Patent-Office Report of 1853, Agriculture, 61, states that the ordinary day's journey of the dromedary of Cabul is sixty miles, but that picked animals will travel one hundred miles a day for several days in succession, their greatest speed being about ten miles an hour. Captain Lyon [1] affirms that the mahari of the Sahara will travel many successive hours at the rate of nine miles an hour. The Syrian deloul goes in five days from Bagḍad to Sokhne, a distance which the loaded caravans require twenty-one days to perform, or from the same city to Aleppo in seven, the caravans generally taking twenty-five. Couriers have ridden, without change of dromedary, from Cairo to Mecca in eighteen days, while the ordinary camels seldom accomplish the journey in less than forty-five. Layard [2] gives several instances

[1] Travels in Africa, 114.

[2] New Researches.

of apparently remarkable performance, but as the distances are not stated, it is not easy to compare them with those recorded by other authors. A late and apparently credible writer says: "I knew a camel-driver who had bought a dromedary belonging to a sherif of Mecca, lately deceased at Cairo. This animal often made the round trip between that city and Suez, going and returning in twenty-four hours, thus travelling a distance of sixty leagues in a single day."[1] The performance of the dromedary is rather understated by the writer. The actual distance between Cairo and Suez is eighty-four English miles, and the animal must consequently have accomplished one hundred and sixty-eight miles in twenty-four hours. He remained four hours at Suez to rest, and therefore travelled at the rate of eight miles and four tenths per hour.

Upon longer journeys, the daily rate of the best dromedaries, though not equal to these instances, is still extraordinary. A French officer of high rank and character in the Egyptian service, assured me that he had ridden a favorite dromedary ninety miles in a single day, and five hundred miles in ten. Mails have been carried from Bagdad to Damascus, upon the same animals, four hundred and eighty-two miles, in

[1] Revue Orientale, I. 280.

seven days; and on one occasion, by means of regular relays, Mehemet Ali sent an express to Ibrahim Pasha, from Cairo to Antioch, five hundred and sixty miles, in five days and a half. But the most remarkable long journey on record is that of Col. Chesney, of the British army, who rode with three companions, and without change of camel, from Basrah to Damascus, a distance of nine hundred and sixty miles, in nineteen days and three or four hours, thus averaging fifty miles per day, the animals having no food but such as they gathered for themselves during the halts of the party. These dromedaries averaged forty-five steps a minute, with a length of step of six feet five inches, giving a speed of about three and one third miles the hour.

In an appendix to the work of Carbuccia, Jomard affirms that a detachment of the celebrated dromedary regiment in the French army of Egypt, marched from Cairo to El-Arish, from El-Arish to Suez, from Suez to Cairo, and from Cairo to Pelusium, a distance in all of not less than six hundred miles in *eight days*, and he adds that the ordinary day's march of the regiment was thirty French leagues, or about seventy-five miles, without a halt. These extraordinary statements rest on the testimony of a single individual, and though the corps was composed wholly of picked animals and picked men, and inspired by the energy of a Bonaparte, I find it quite impossible to give them full credence.

The Bactrian certainly does not possess the speed of the Arabian deloul or the African mahari, but he is used extensively, and with great advantage, in high northern latitudes, as a beast of the saddle. He is ridden through all the vast territory where he occurs, except in Cabul and the Crimea, and, as we have seen above, is capable of travelling from fifty to sixty-five miles in a day, a rate of performance quite equal to that of the common dromedary. In the winter especially, as Bergmann says, they are preferable to horses, because they are more sure-footed, and the length of their legs enables them to travel with ease in a depth of snow where a horse could scarcely move at all. Their gait under the saddle appears to resemble that of the Arabian, the light amble, according to Bergmann, being easy, while the swifter pace violently tosses the rider.

The *regular* gaits of the camel are all properly paces or ambles, that is, he does not move his legs, like most other quadrupeds, *per diametrum*, but lifts the fore and hinder feet of the same side at nearly the same time. When hotly pursued by cavalry, he breaks into an awkward gallop, but this movement, which is a rapid one, can be kept up but a short time. Carbuccia says, p. 21, "a horse upon the gallop is quickly distanced by the dromedary on the gallop," and again p. 129, "they gallop well, and there is no soldier who has not seen horsemen pursue them at full speed without overtaking them." Jomard, in the appendix before quoted, says, "the swiftest horses are outstripped at last by the dromedary, which, starting with a long trot, equals the speed of the horse, and finally comes up with him." Bergmann, as quoted by Ritter,[1] speaking apparently of the Bactrian of the Calmucks, states, that when they are galloping, entirely at liberty, no horseman can overtake them. Burckhardt, on the contrary,[2] declares that the speed of the dromedary never approaches, even for short distances, that of the common horse, and that he cannot maintain his swiftest pace for more than half an hour. When we consider that this traveller was familiar with the Berber dromedaries and with those of Nedjd, which are acknowledged to be the swiftest breeds, and especially when we compare the structure and habitual movements of the two animals, we can scarcely fail to conclude that his testimony is worthy of more confidence than the conflicting evidence I have cited. I witnessed a dromedary race at the camp of an Arab Sheikh in the Sinaïtic peninsula. About a dozen animals, mostly young,

1 Erdkunde, XIII. 692.

2 Bedouins, 263.

contended for the victory, and as I have before remarked, their noses were slit the day before, by way of preparation. The course was not above two or three hundred yards, and so much time was lost in starting and turning, that though they went at a prodigious rate over the centre of the course, it was difficult to form any estimate of their speed as compared with that of the horse. The race presented a very animated picture, and the shrill shouts of the ambitious riders, the apparent rivalry of the animals, and the peculiar *ululatus* of the women, which the Arabs pretend is produced by a rapid *lateral* vibration of the tongue, gave the whole scene a very wild and exciting character.

From the great length of step, the motion of the burden camel and the slow walk of the dromedary are necessarily violent, and at first very wearisome to the rider; but a few days practice accustoms him to this rough exercise, and he performs his day's journey with as little exhaustion as upon horseback. "Although mounted on an animal capable of much fleeter motion," says a writer in the American Whig Review, whom we have before quoted, "the traveller is, in general, obliged to conform to the snail's pace of the caravan, because he cannot with convenience, or indeed at all times with safety, be separated from his baggage and attendants; but if he is content to dispense with the comforts of tents, camp-bedsteads and stools, and folding tables, and to subsist on the simple fare of the Arabs, he may traverse the wilderness at a far more rapid rate."

"Most travellers complain of camel-riding as a peculiarly wearisome and unpleasant mode of locomotion; but with these fastidious persons I can by no means agree; and as compared with the

> Pack-horses, and hollow, pampered jades of Asia,
> That cannot go but thirty miles a day,

whereof we had large experience in the hill country of Palestine and the parts adjacent,[1] my party all unhesitatingly gave the camel the preference. Of course, on a good road, neither too soft nor too hard, where you may choose your pace, walk, jog-trot, amble or gallop your beast, avail yourself of

> ——tolutation,
> As they do term't, or succussation,

just as jumps best with your humor; the horse, I will not deny, is a better vehicle than the camel, in respect of fatigue at least, in the same pro-

1 The reader will find a very faithful description of the horses usually furnished Frank travellers in Syria, in the history of the gazelle hunt, in Mr. G. Ross Browne's very lively and amusing Yusef, or a Crusade in the East.

portion that the hippogriff is better than either; but excepting the space between Cairo and Suez, you will not find many roods of such road in the Deserts of Libya, nor yet in Araby the Stony, or even the Blest. In fact, the great Macadam, the colossus of Roads, does not appear as yet to have visited the greater or the lesser Peninsula, which therefore remain much in the same condition that man was before 'the social compact,' namely, in a state of nature."

Tavernier observes, that the quick amble of the dromedary is easier than his walk, and Bergmann makes a similar remark. Burckhardt,[1] speaking of the fine dromedaries of the upper Nile, says they are unequalled for ease to the rider when allowed to take their own pace, an amble of five, or five and a half miles the hour, and the Arabs apply to them a proverbial expression, "his gait is so soft that you may drink a cup of coffee while you ride him." A day's journey of fifty or sixty miles at this pace is an easy achievement. At much more rapid rates, however, the motion becomes again intolerably violent, and an inexperienced rider finds it almost impossible to cling to the saddle, or even to catch his breath, though at the ordinary speed the seat is more secure than on horseback.

[1] Bedouins, 263.

Jomard, citing the authority of Col. Prétot, says that the violent motion of the animals of the dromedary corps sometimes brought on a spitting of blood in the riders, and although Carbuccia denies, what has been often affirmed, that the movement produces a nausea like sea-sickness, Burnes, it will be remembered, travelling in a *kajawah*, experienced this inconvenience. "The rider of the mahari," says Daumas,[1] "strengthens himself by two very tight belts or girdles, one about the loins and abdomen, the other under the armpits."

The security of the seat, though at once *felt* by all who have mounted the camel, seems hardly reconcilable with the violence of his motion, and is not easily explained; but nothing is more rare than a fall from his back, except when he is moving at a much more rapid pace than his ordinary amble of five miles an hour or thereabouts. A writer already more than once quoted, says: "To me, who am no graduate of Astley's, and so sorry an equestrian that I respect Alexander more for the taming of Bucephalus than for the conquest of India, this *security* is a great point; you may sit sidewise or backwards, with feet resting in stirrups, or legs crossed or dangling, and arms folded or akimbo, with no fear that your beast will kick up or stumble and pitch you over his

[1] Mœurs et coutumes de l'Algérie, 354.

head, or rear and throw you over his tail, or shy out from under you at the sight of an old woman or the bow of a country school-boy, or take the bit in his teeth and run to Quoddy with you, at the 'report of a caliver' or the flutter of a sheep-skin; but nevertheless, with a full sense of my responsibilities, I do take it upon me to deny the boast of some, that they can use a telescope, read write, and cipher, sew, knit, darn stockings, and even draw, *a-camelback*. The motion of the beast is a compound of rolling and pitching simultaneously executed, and much resembles that of a very short 'dug out' with a strong, rough current abeam, and a sharp heavy swell fore and aft. The elder Pliny, who read and dictated not only in his chariot, but even while *shampooing*, would have been compelled to intermit his lucubrations during a promenade *à chameau;* and though the Arab will hang like a sack across the pack-saddle, or stretch himself from stem to stern along the load, and sleep as securely as a bear in a hollow log, or a sailor in the main-top, the most you can accomplish, fair madam, will be to look about you, which you can do to good purpose, while your hands are as useless as if they were tied to the cross-head of a mill-saw."

Every oriental traveller can testify that the Arabs often sleep upon their camels when on the march,[1] and Colonel Chesney [2] and Layard give curious accounts of the preparation and even cooking of food on the backs of the camels by the Arab women, during forced marches. During a retreat, one woman mounted on a camel loaded with grain, grinds the wheat in a hand-mill; the flour is passed to another riding an animal that carries the water-sacks; she mixes and kneads the dough, and passes it to a third, who bakes it in a portable oven or chafing-dish heated with wood or straw. The milking of the female camels is performed with equal facility and as little delay, and thus the march is kept up, without a halt, as long as the animals are able to travel.

1 Burckhardt, *Arabia*, 312, describes the robbers who lie in wait for the caravans as jumping up behind the riders when they are asleep, and pillaging the loading; and in the same volume, page 314, he observes that the camels are accustomed to stop when their masters fall asleep.

2 Expedition to the Euphrates, II. 671.

# CHAPTER XIII.

## THE CARAVAN.

"For the purposes of general observation, camel-riding is the most advantageous of all possible means of conveyance. The slowness and regularity of your rate of progress, the elevation of your seat, which gives you a wide range of vision, and (no trifling matter in the parched desert) secures you the full benefit of every breeze that blows, and your entire exemption from the necessity of guiding or even watching the movements of your beast, afford you the greatest facilities for studying the aspect of the country, and enjoying the unrivalled sublimity of the mountain ranges which in the Arabian and most other deserts, you so often skirt or traverse. With a special attendant too, whom you can call upon to pick up a stone, or gather some curious plant, or, upon occasion, to bring your camel to a halt, that you may take a sketch or record an observation, or dismount and examine for yourself some tempting vein of mineral or other interesting object, you will have every opportunity for observing and noting in detail, and thus enjoy a combination of advantages hardly attainable in any other mode of travel. Such an attendant is almost indispensable if you desire to make botanical or mineralogical collections, or if you aim at anything beyond a mere general view of the phenomena by which you are surrounded. Without him, you will hardly be able to stop your beast[1] until after you have lost sight of the flower or mineral that has attracted you, and if you finally succeed in overcoming his repugnance to lag behind the rest of the caravan, and persuading him to kneel and let you dismount, he will be sure to be up and away while you are gone back for your treasure, leaving you to pant after him when you have satisfied your curiosity or bagged your specimen. Again, the wadys through which your road lies are sometimes of considerable width, and as the camel chooses his path without any reference to the picturesque, it may happen that some other route would better suit your view-hunting propensities. In this case, you cannot readily rein him out of the track as you might a horse, and then make up for lost time by following on at a gallop. Any deviation from the beaten path costs you, first, a hard struggle with your self-willed beast, and then, if you prevail upon

[1] Burckhardt, *Syria*, 445. "The camel cannot be stopped while his companions are moving."

him to go *your* way, you soon find yourself separated from your company by a greater distance than is always agreeable in *partibus infidelium*. Major Skinner saith, 'A thick cherry stick, with a cross at the end of it, serves to guide the animal; a gentle tap on the right side of his neck sends him to the left, and one on the opposite side turns him back to the right; to make him move quicker, prick him with the point of the stick on the shoulders; a knock on the back of the neck stops him, and a few blows between the ears, accompanied by a certain guttural sound resembling the Arabic letter *khe*, bring him to his knees.' With a well-trained beast, 'a thick cherry stick with a cross at the end of it,' in the hands of a Bedouin, and, I am bound to believe, in the valiant Major's, will work wonders, but not in yours, madam, nor in mine."

"The frequented routes in the desert, wherever the soil is not too hard to receive or too soft permanently to retain impressions, are furrowed with paths which may have been thousands of years in wearing. In the Sinaïtic peninsula, where, except on the Hadj, a great pilgrim route, the caravans are usually small, there are (in the narrower passes excepted) in general from fifteen to twenty of these shallow paths worn smooth in the hard gravel and among the loose stones. They are fifteen or eighteen inches wide, and three, four, or more deep, and, though occasionally intersecting, running in the main parallel to each other at the distance of two or three yards apart. An Arabian poem, older than the time of Mohammed, compares these paths to the stripes of a parti-colored cloak; and the Arabian traveller of the present day finds the same resemblance between the face of the desert and the 'many-colored coat' of its more opulent inhabitants. In these paths, the camels walk usually pretty nearly abreast if not too numerous, and those which have been bred together are inclined to keep near each other. Where there is pasturage, they scatter widely, and a company of fifty camels in a broad wady will frequently extend themselves to a front of a mile or more. They are however very reluctant to lose sight of the main body, and, as has been before noticed, it is difficult to stop one of these animals before the time of encamping, and while the rest of the caravan is upon the march. Notwithstanding this gregarious propensity, it is not easy to keep two camels in a caravan side by side, so as to allow much conversation between their riders. Some difference in gait, the temptations of a camel-thorn or a thistle, or the crowding of other animals, are constantly interfering to break up your *tête-à-tête*, and you finally surrender yourself to a silence well befitting the solitude and the solemn aspect of nature around you. The regular and noiseless tread of the camel, and the faint rustling of the sand, as it rolls back to the cavity left by the foot of the animal, shed a drowsy influence on your reveries; your day-dreams melt into slumberous visions; you waver in your seat, and it is rather an instinctive impulse than a conscious effort, that braces you in your saddle, and saves you from a disastrous fall."

The Arabs habitually travel much by night, and this not, as has been supposed, for the sake of the guidance of the stars, which they seldom need, but partly to avoid the greater heat of the day, and more especially to allow the camel, which never feeds by night, the daylight for gathering his food. By travelling a part of the night, too, they can make a long march, and yet arrive at the proposed station by daylight, and thus avoid the inconvenience of pitching the camp, collecting fuel and water, and cooking their evening meal, in the dark. It is common to start from midnight to two o'clock, and to march, without halting, ten, fifteen, or sometimes twenty hours, after which the camp is formed; and if it is not yet dark, the camels are turned out to graze till sunset, when they return to the camp, are hobbled, by tying up one of the folded fore legs, and ruminate and sleep to the hour of departure. Although so long a day's journey without pause is fatiguing to the rider, yet, except with light dromedaries, experience is in favor of the practice. To halt without unloading the camels would afford them no relief, but fatigue them the more by practically lengthening their day's work; and if they are unloaded and allowed to wander in search of food, the time lost in collecting them and rearranging their burdens would bring the caravan too late to the camping-ground. Where, however, the party, as is the case with military expeditions of a few days' length, is unaccompanied by burden camels, and the dromedaries are loaded with only the equipage, water, and provisions of their riders, the hours of travel and repose can, without inconvenience, be arranged and varied to suit the exigencies of the occasion.

The following account of the organization of a caravan, and the every-day incidents of desert travel, is introduced from the unpublished journal, before referred to, not as possessing special merit, but as containing some useful hints for persons about to undertake excursions of that character.

"If you have well and diligently perused and digested my first number, reader, you are now possessed of some tithe of my painfully gathered stock of learning concerning the camel, and if you will go along with me in my somewhat devious wanderings, I will use with you as much familiarity as is good betwixt teacher and pupil, and will incidentally impart to you, with other pleasant and profitable knowledges, such store of further information on that topic, that, among people who know no better, you shall come at last to be thought very nearly as wise as your master.

"According to my 'unheedful vow,' I am now to introduce you to the Desert and the Bedouins; but before I proceed to describe the wilderness and its inhabitants, it is fit that I convey you fairly into the midst of them; and therefore we will first organize our caravan, and then mount our dromedaries and pace forth a day's journey into the waste, after which we will sit cosily down together, compare notes, and draw up a description of the sights and sounds which have struck most strangely upon our inexperienced eye and ear.

"Having engaged your 'guide, philosopher, and friend,' the dragoman, your next business is, with the aid of that personage and the consul, to contract with some potent sheikh for the safe and convenient conveyance of yourself and your luggage *through the territory of his tribe*,—mark that; for without special license, hard to be obtained, he can go no further; and when he has set you down at the end of his tether, you must make the best bargain you can with the next sheikh; or, if he proves too hard a customer for you, you must (many as pretty a man as you hath done it before you) e'en turn back again the way you came. The transportation of European travellers is a source of great profit to the Arabs, and every tribe jealously reserves to itself the exclusive right to this lucrative employment within its own limits. The sheikhs not unfrequently undertake to smuggle caravans across each other's territories, but if detected in the attempt, they are sure to be resisted unto blood; and it is not above three or four years since a sheikh, who was thus breaking his neighbour's close, with a company of English travellers, between Mount Sinai and Akaba, being met by a party of the offended tribe, was led aside into a thicket and butchered on the spot. On these occasions, violence is seldom offered to the traveller, unless he is foolish enough to provoke it, but he is exposed to much annoyance and delay, and his effects are likely to be roughly handled in the *melée*.

" But let us come back to our contract. Your Arab sheikh, though a gentleman of an ancient house, is a great adept at driving a bargain, and during the operation, he imbibes (at the cost of his customer) a monstrous quantity of coffee and tobacco smoke, much in the same way, and for the same purpose, as a Yankee 'whittles a stick' in swapping horses. You must draw your contract as carefully as with an Italian vetturino; and you may be very sure that if in the course of your journey you ask any deviation from the route, delay, or other indulgence 'not i' the bond,' you will have a good round price to pay for it. Upon concluding the bargain, you usually pay a part of the sum stipulated, in advance, and when at the end of your journey the sheikh comes to your tent to make his last salaam and receive your final compliments, he will again remind you of your old friend the vetturino, by a request for a *teskereh*, (Hibernice, 'character,') and a very significant hint, that he cannot believe you sincere in the expression of your satisfaction with his services and attentions, unless you seal your testimony with a *backsheesh*.

"You are now to procure your tents and other camp equipage and travelling gear, as well as your supplies, and, thanks to English love of comfort, you will find in all the great towns in the vicinity of the Desert every facility for making the journey not only conveniently but luxuriously. English travellers have introduced a multitude of portable contrivances in the way of camp-furniture, and by the aid of these and with due foresight in laying in your stores, you may spend a few weeks in the Desert with as little of real privation or discomfort of any sort, as in ordinary travelling in America or Europe. In general, the Desert furnishes no supplies, except now and then a sheep at an exorbitant price, or, if you are a sportsman, occasionally a gazelle, a mountain goat, (beden,) a hare, or a partridge; but at Suez, Mount Sinai, Akaba, and the Oases, you find bread, coffee, eggs, Arab cheese, and sometimes vegetables. The necessity of taking along with you these stores, as well as your camp equipage and cooking utensils, and a supply of water for several days' journey, obliges you to engage a great many camels, and you will be fortunate if you are not made to pay for a considerably larger number than are really needed for the purpose. The loads are seldom weighed, and the superior knowledge of the Arab as to the burden his camel really ought to carry gives him an advantage over the traveller, which it is pretty difficult to resist.

"Your luggage and stores being at last packed in trunks, canteen-boxes, sacks, and palm-leaf crates, or *cafasses*, and with much vehement altercation, shrill shouting, and passionate gesticulation of the Bedouins, infinite growling of their blatant beasts, and alternate coaxing and scolding of your dragoman, fairly loaded and secured with ropes and netting, you must look to your dromedary, and see that your saddle and appurtenances are arranged to your liking; and here let me caution you to be sure that every convenience you can need in the course of the day's journey is hung to your saddle-pegs or stored in the ample travelling-bags beneath you. Of these conveniences, one of the most indispensable is the *zemzeméeh*, or leather water-bottle. This is a neatly made water-vessel, usually of Russia leather, holding a couple of quarts, with a large neck and a wooden stopper. It is very important, that both this and the water casks and water skins, should have been soaked for several days, and often filled and emptied, both to make them tight and to take out a little of the raw taste of the wood and leather. The *zemzeméeh* is hung by a strap and hook to the saddle-peg, and as some of the water escapes by exudation through the pores of the leather, the evaporation cools the contents, upon the same principle as in the porous earthen jars, so extensively used in Egypt and other hot countries. The *zemzeméeh* should always be hung on the shady side of the camel, and well sheltered by the carpets or other coverings of your saddle, and with these precautions, the water will be cool enough in the hottest weather, though it must be confessed, that it will always taste of the leather, at least as strongly as Sancho Panza's grandfather's wine did of iron and goat's skin, from the little key and its thong, that had been dropped into the hogshead. As to the use of the water-bottle, I have but two pieces of advice to give you. One is to keep it out of the way of the Arabs, who will seize every opportunity to drain it, and the other is to have recourse to it as sparingly as possible while on the march.[1] The habit of frequent indulgence in this respect provokes thirst, and a little self-denial at the beginning will save you a good deal of suffering afterwards, when your stock of water is spoiled or exhausted. For water skins and water bottles, india rubber (provided you don't object to a spice of brimstone) is a better material than leather, though the *zemzeméeh*, on account of the transpiration, is cooler, but you will find no 'elastics' in the East, and must procure your receptacles of the Neptunian fluid from one of the great rival Vulcanists, Day or Goodyear, before leaving home."

[1] Major Denham made it a rule never to drink at all between sunrise and sunset, but at night he drank "as much water as he could swallow." The Arabs do not abstain upon the march, but are constantly drinking through the day. But this is merely the improvidence and thoughtlessness of savages, and argues nothing for the practice.

## CHAPTER XIV.

### THE CARAVAN, CONTINUED.

"But I had forgotten to give you some advice respecting your travelling garb. Let us repair this omission before we mount our dromedaries and plunge into the wilderness. The night is generally cool, often even cold, in the desert, and for the early morning you will require a sufficient supply of warm wrappages, though for the rest of the day, except, of course, in the winter, thin summer clothing only is necessary. The most difficult point is to defend the head against the powerful rays of the sun, and to protect the face and lips from the parching wind. The Bedouins usually wear only a close fitting skull-cap, and a large silk handkerchief, called the *kefeeyeh.* The kefeeyeh is woven in broad stripes, yellow and red being the favorite colors, and with a very long, but thin, fringe. It is folded shawl-wise, and worn over the cap, the long folded edge in front. This edge is brought very far forward, a braided or twisted woollen band, sometimes very tastefully fashioned, passes around the head and confines the handkerchief, and the corners hang free, or are gathered about the neck. This is a very tolerable protection for the face, but Europeans would find it insufficient for the crown, and in the heat of the day, the Arab himself very often wraps his head in the folds of an ample turban, a thick woollen blanket, or the skirt of his *bernoos*, or cloak. I found the East Indian *pith* hat, with a quilted cotton cover, and when the long narrow cotton shawl, called *kushack* in Egypt, thrown over it in thick folds, gathered about the neck, and knotted under the chin, the best head-gear. The kushack both prevents the light hat from blowing off, and effectually shields the head, face, and lips from sun and wind; and this plan seemed to me much preferable to any European head-dress, because it relieves you from that great annoyance, the necessity of carrying and looking after a heavy umbrella. You, reader, I have every reason to believe, are a very nice person, and therefore, remembering that the washerwoman is not yet abroad in the desert, you will, I trust, take along with you good store of clean linen, and listen not at all to the authority or the example of the author of the 'Hastily gobbled up Crudities,' who held him guilty of sinful superfluity that 'had more suits or shirts than bodies,' or of the nasty Frenchman Laborde, who allows you 'three shirts' for a two months' trip, and even found *one* quite sufficient for himself. Many of the desert plateaus lie at a considerable elevation, and the nights and mornings are sometimes very cool, even in summer. A good *bernoos*, or *poncho*, or other convenient wraprascal is therefore no superfluity, and in general the Mississippi summer costume (shirt, bowie-knife, revolver and spurs,) is not to be affected. The violent motion of the camel requires freedom of habiliment, and all your vesture should be wide. Further, go not thinly shod. The edge of the sandstone is sharper than a serpent's tooth, and thick soles are *de rigueur*. Your shaving apparatus you may leave behind altogether. Not that I approve beard and mustache, but they are a protection against the scorching sun, and besides, two or three shaves of a sandy beard will hack the edge of your razor like Falstaff's sword, and thereafter shaving is impossible. I would fain add some special counsels touching ladies' apparel, but though I have answered to the name of 'Benedick, the married man,' more years than I care to confess in this presence, and though my faithful Joan hath interspersed her curtain lectures to her Darby, with sundry prelections on this very topic, yet, as a man may say, I have profited nothing by them, and do profess a respectful ignorance of the whole subject to this day, not knowing the difference between a gore and a gusset. Nathless, I comfort myself with the consideration, that feminine ingenuity passeth all masculine imagination, and I do in nowise doubt, that these few hints, with a repetition of a former suggestion, that you, madam, may find it convenient to ride *à chevauchons*, will enable you to devise a garb at once graceful, durable, and commodious, beyond anything which the subtlest man-milliner could compose.

"But the dragoman is sounding 'boot and saddle,' after his fashion, our camels are laden, our dromedaries are waiting, not indeed champing the bit and pawing the ground like fiery coursers, but with half-shut eye lazily 'chewing the cud of sweet and bitter fancy.' Let us mount our ungainly steeds and away to the desert.

"The camel, as every body knows, kneels to receive his load and his rider, and the burden he can rise with is said to be the measure of what he is able to carry. The Bedouins often climb to the saddle, without bringing the camel to his knees or even stopping him, by putting one foot on the callus of the knee, and so clambering up by the neck and shoulder, but I recommend no such experiments to you. You will find mounting in the ordinary way ticklish enough in the beginning, and you run considerable risk at first of going off by a very illogical, *à priori*, or *à posteriori* movement, as the animal rises. It is a 'bad eminence' to fall from, and until you have had considerable practice in this sort of slack-rope exercise, it is good to hold fast by the saddle-pins both fore and aft, while the dromedary is unfolding his joints, and working his traverse upwards. Further, see that your attendant keeps one foot on your camel's knee until you are well posited and balanced; for he is apt to start up on feeling the weight of his rider, and in this case you may very likely go up on one side and come down on the other. When all is ready, you give the signal, your Arab releases the camel, a sudden jerk from behind pitches you upon the pommel as he raises his haunches, (for, as we told you before, he comes up stern foremost,) and then a swell from the stem throws you aft, and so on, zigzag, until he is fairly up, when, after a little more rolling, while he is poising and steadying, backing and filling, and getting his feet into marching order, he steps off, and you are at last under way, on your quest for Mesopotamia, Arabia Petræa, or the Oasis of Jupiter Ammon.

"Your first day is every where a *dies non*,

and reason good. It takes many hours to collect the camels and their drivers for the first time, and there is many a dispute to settle as to whether Achmed's or Musa's camel shall carry this or that parcel of luggage; and then, as many things are sure to be forgotten on starting, it is good to lodge the first night within hail of your point of departure, so that things missing may be brought out of limbo, and new-found wants supplied from town without too much loss of time. Your tent and camp equipage have been sent out to the appointed station before you, and on arriving, after an hour's ride, you find all things in order, so that this time you do not witness the pitching of the camp, and your real experience of desert life does not begin till to-morrow.

"Your first night under canvas passes very comfortably, disturbed by nothing but the quarrels of the Arabs about the division of the expected profits, or perhaps some slight rustling under your pillow or about your bed, ominously like the crawling of a scorpion or the wriggle of a snake. You will wisely have ordered breakfast to be ready as early as you can see to eat it, (and if 'by the misty moonbeams' struggling light,' or by 'lanterns dimly burning,' so much the better,) in order that you may start in time to reach your next station before the hottest hours of the day. The preparing and partaking of breakfast, breaking up the camp, packing the luggage and loading the camels, consumes about two hours, and therefore if you mean to be off, ere

Phibbus' car
Doth shine from far,

you must stir and *conclamare vasa* betimes.

"As the camel regularly is fed only at night, he is impatient for his morning's meal, which he picks up for himself from the shrubs that dot the desert, and takes, as hypocritical old Seneca pretends (falsely, I doubt,) he did his, *sine mensa.* Each animal makes off as soon as he is loaded, and as the loads frequently require to be re-secured or otherwise changed, and the camels scatter widely in search of food, it is some time before the caravan is collected, and steadily advancing in regular order.

"When the country is safe, and the order of march fairly established, and all is going on smoothly, the sheikhs and others who have dromedaries, often pace ahead of the caravan, in order to gain time for a cup of coffee and a pipe, or an hour's nap in the shade of an acacia or a manna bush, which they may very well do, as the speed of the dromedary is nearly double that of the ordinary burden camel. I earnestly advise you not to stop the caravan for the foolish purpose of lunching, or to make any halt in the course of the day's march, except such as you can snatch in the way I have just mentioned. It is fair to admit, that the majority of my fellow-travellers are against me on this point, but *n'importe*, wisdom is better than numbers. Hear my reasons; those of mine opponents I need not give. Why should I perplex you?

"For mere lunching, (faugh! I hate the word,) if lunch you must, an orange or two, a biscuit, a morsel of bread, a bunch of dried figs, dates, apricots, or such other pretty little tiny kickshaws, as you can take in your saddle-bags, and munch on your camel, are abundantly sufficient, and as for resting, I know no better way than now and then to exchange your camel for that 'horse with ten toes,' upon which, according to old Fuller, Tom Coryate, memorable for the introduction of forks into England, enterprised his journey to India. To walking, however, there is sometimes a pretty serious objection, the provocation of increased thirst, namely. When you are travelling in hot weather, and your supply of water is low or spoiled, this difficulty becomes nearly insurmountable, and if there be an absolute necessity for stopping, you must prick ahead and gain time, or lag in the rear. A general halt of the caravan is attended with great inconvenience. Barely stopping, without unloading, affords no relief to the camels. On the contrary, it lengthens their day's journey, and of course their fatigue, brings them late to the evening station, and deprives them of the necessary time for feeding and rest. In these annoyances your servants, too, share. They have a hard day's labor to perform, after yours is at an end. They assist in pitching the camp, and unloading the dromedaries. They make your beds, arrange your furniture, attend to your numerous wants, gather fuel, prepare and serve up your dinner, and make the necessary arrangements for an early breakfast, after all which they take their own repast, and make their humble preparations for a repose, which must be interrupted before nature is half refreshed. Besides this, a delay of a couple of hours, either compels you to travel during the hottest part of the day, or, if your halt extends beyond this, you do not reach your camp until evening, and then your dinner comes at an hour when you ought to be seeking in sleep a renewal of strength for the fatigues of the morrow." "When the way is plain, or in moonlight nights, the Arabs sleep through the heat of the day, and travel a large part of the night; but this inversion of the order of nature conduces little to the health or comfort of Europeans and Americans, who like to take their sleep *cool;* and besides, it defeats in a measure one great object of your journey, the view of the wonderful scenery of the Desert.

"The usual length of a day's march is from eight to twelve hours, and the stations are selected with reference to the convenience of obtaining fodder, water, and fuel. The Arabs prefer the regular and familiar places of encampment, but they are objectionable on account of the vermin which frequent them, and the traveller should see that his tent is pitched on ground that does not show the 'one spot of ashen black,' the usual sign of recent occupation.

"Towards the close of the march, the sheikhs and other experienced travellers hasten on in advance of the caravan, to select the ground for the camp, and when a level spot is found spacious enough to accommodate the tents and camels, and within convenient distance of some scattering thicket of shrubs, which promises wood for the fire, and feed for the beasts, the leading sheikh dismounts and plants his spear. The camels seem to understand this manœuvre, and when they come in sight of the spear, and their brethren kneeling around it, they quicken their pace, and speedily join the weary group. As the camels come up, they are made to kneel, unloaded, and turned out to feed. Carpets and cushions are spread for the traveller in the scanty shade of some thinly leafed shrub, the tents of the Franks (for the Arabs use none except in their stationary camps) are unpacked and pitched, their beds, camp-stools, and other conveniences are duly disposed, dry wood is gathered, fires and pipes are lighted, and coffee, (probably stolen from your own stores,) frequently highly flavoured with cloves or other pungent spices, is politely sent you by the principal sheikh of the caravan, and then come the cookery, the dinner, and the preparations for the night.

"When the camels return from feeding, which is towards sunset, they are made to lie down about the tents, and generally secured by tying up one of the fore legs. The Arabs sit, smoke, and talk awhile around the fire, and then, wrapping up in their blankets or tattered cloaks, they stretch themselves on the ground and compose themselves to sleep. The sheikhs fare no better than their followers, except that they carry a carpet or two, a more liberal supply of clothing, and some other trifling conveniences which the common Bedouins cannot afford. Bread is almost the sole diet of the Arabs, when travelling, but the *honoratiores* among them are very apt to take the liberty of intruding themselves upon the hospitality of your poor servants, as they are consuming the relics of your repast, and in this case they are pretty sure to secure to themselves the lion's share. It is always stipulated that the Arabs shall furnish their own food and water, but they rarely provide themselves with a sufficient supply of either; and as they are bold, persevering, and importunate beggars, it is very difficult to protect your stores against their rapacity.

"And now that we have got well through our first day in the Desert, and are fairly out of sight of land, let me sit down on the shady side of the tent, and while our tardy dinner is preparing, talk over the experiences of the day, and write up our journals. And, here let me impress on the present reader, and I hope future traveller, the extreme importance of keeping a most full and minute record of every observation and every noteworthy occurrence. I have heard and read a great deal in my time on memories; and been told how, forsooth, people who can't read and write, and so make no notes, and don't relax their memorial muscles by using artificial supports, and leaning on broken reeds of memorandum books and lead pencils, have much more retentive memories than those who avail themselves of such unnatural substitutes. Believe me, reader, 'tis all moonshine. You remember no whit the worse, and you observe vastly better, for the practice of full, clear, and accurate description. In travelling in strange lands, where all—nature, art, man—is new, the continual succession of novel objects is unfavorable for obtaining distinct and above all permanent impressions, and the most tenacious memory can hope to retain but a small proportion of the images received. It is wonderful how the perusal of a good book of travels over the same ground, or a glance at your journal, if reasonably full, will refresh and revive the fading pictures, which it has cost you so much time and toil to obtain, and scarcely any sacrifice is too great to secure an object so important. Let no excuse of lassitude, no impatience of the inconveniences of writing on your knee in the open air, with insects buzzing about your ears, and the wind scattering your papers and sanding your page before it is filled, deter you from conscientiously setting down every thing that has struck you during the day as worthy of being seen. Trust nothing to the memory. Make no vague entries, such as 'fine scenery after sunrise,' 'remarkable rock far off to the right,' 'singular appearance in the sky this morning,' and so forth, foolishly imagining that you will remember the details, and have the energy to write them out to-morrow. Making a matter 'the order of the day, for to-morrow, amounts, in congressional language and practice, to indefinite postponement. You will find, too late, that it has the same signification in your itinerant vocabulary. I once heard a motion to that effect objected to by a 'new member,' on the ground that to-morrow was Sunday. In your case, there is a more valid exception. To-morrow will bring with it new observations to record, new inconveniences to surmount, new weariness to combat, and what is not worth securing to-day will have even less value to-morrow.

"Let us, then, resolutely make a clean breast of it, and faithfully record the impressions of the day; and depend upon it, both we and the world shall be the wiser for it."

# CHAPTER XV.

## NUMBERS OF THE CAMEL — ORIENTAL EXAGGERATION.

The wealth of all pastoral tribes consists in their cattle, and as in the desert the camel contributes in a larger share to supply the wants of the household than any other animal, he is naturally the measure of poverty and affluence. The number of camels required to maintain their possessor in comfort is by no means large. With ten or fewer camels, says Chesney, an Arab is poor; with thirty or forty, in easy circumstances; with sixty, rich. Among civilized nations the possession of land is in general a condition precedent to the acquisition of flocks, but in the desert, where all the soil within the purlieus of the tribe is common property, the youth who is ambitious of rising in the world need give himself no trouble to become a freeholder. Of late years, the utility, price, and profits of the camel, in all the deserts bordering upon the Mediterranean, have greatly increased, from the demand for his services in transporting goods between Cairo and Suez, and travellers from Egypt to Palestine, as well as in the rapidly extending commerce between the North African seaports and central Africa. These varied sources of gain are no doubt more than an equivalent for the loss sustained by the reduced numbers of the pilgrim caravans to Mecca, for though as many camels are not now at any one time required, yet the demand extends through the year, and the prices paid for conveyance and transportation are much higher than they formerly were.

The multiplication of the camels possessed by a sheikh or a tribe, finds natural limits and checks in the difficulty of procuring an adequate supply of fodder for more than a certain number, within the territory of the tribe, and of protecting the animals against the thieves who are always lurking about the frontier to pick up estrays, or to make a bold dash and drive off a herd. The desert camels are branded, usually on the neck and left shoulder, every tribe and every family having its own mark, not so much to enable the owner to recognize a beast which may have been eloigned from him, and which he knows by natural tokens as well as if it were his child, but to serve as an evidence of property by which he may establish his rights, to the satisfaction of others.

Raids and forays, for the purpose of stealing horses and camels, are nowise disreputable among the Arabs, and enterprising adventurers do not always inquire very nicely, whether their own tribe and that on which they propose to make a descent are technically at peace, or according to the *jus gentium* in such a state of hostility, that reprisals for old offences or new provocations may be justified. The moss troopers, if observed, are of course resisted, and these filibustering expeditions, and the blood-feuds which grow out of them, are a never-ending cause of war between the Bedouin tribes.

The harmonizing effects of commerce are very plainly seen in all the relations between the Bedouins and Europeans. The Arab still thinks, no doubt, with Aymerigot Marcel, that "to pille and to robbe is a fayre and goode lyfe, alle thynges considered," yet as a regular vocation, he finds it not so safe, or, in the long run, so profitable, to plunder Franks as to pilot them through the desert. There have, accordingly, been but few recent instances of open violence to travellers, in any part of the East where Arabs are often brought into contact with Europeans, although it must be confessed that cases of pilfering are not altogether so rare, and the Bedouins themselves not unfrequently dispute, sword in hand, the possession of the traveller. I borrow from the often quoted journal the following description of one of these quarrels:—

"The Arabs were almost constantly at loggerheads among themselves. Their wars were chiefly of words, and it is incredible what a power of lungs they will exhibit on a question of two pence. While with them, we had among our own Bedouins, besides several minor and more informal set-tos and one general *melée* in which the belligerents did little but push each other about, one regular *duello, dans les formes*, with swords. The dispute was about furnishing camels for the Hawajees, but I did not inquire into the precise point of difference. Why should I pester myself with the quarrels of Ethnicks? Nevertheless, I felt a good deal of interest in the result. I shall tell you why. One of the combatants had a short-bladed sword, true Damascus, with a chased silver hilt, which I had in vain tempted him to sell. But no, it had been his father's, and *his* father's, and so on back to Adnan, from whom all Bedouins are descended. I hoped that, in a certain event, his administrator would be less scrupulous. The champions were placed in the centre of a ring of Arabs, and when all was ready, 'winked and held out their cold iron.' After a little preliminary flourishing, they went at their good work in earnest. They poked, they cut, they thrust, and they parried, in tierce, in carte, and in sundry other curves not hitherto investigated by mathematicians, or the masters of the noble science of defence, until my friend of the short sword received a sufficient flesh wound in the leg, (alas! not mortal,) whereupon certain officious and pragmatical reformers then and there present interfered, and separated the doughty paladins, to the great scandal of sundry old Bedouins of the camp, who, one and all, declared that this uncalled for intervention was a most unwarrantable infraction of the ancient laws of honorable warfare, as understood and practised from time immemorial among the sons of Ishmael."

In spite of the apparent difficulty of procuring sustenance for large herds in parched climates and barren soils, the number of camels employed by the governments and the population of Egypt and other Mussulman countries, is incredibly great, and the wandering tribes who occupy regions of comparatively abundant pasturage, possess vast herds of them. On the road between Cairo and Suez you meet many hundreds every day, and the whole Hadj route from Suez to Mecca is strown with their skeletons. I was told at Osioot, that a caravan from Sennaar, which had lately arrived at that place, consisted of six thousand camels. The Mecca pilgrim caravan from Cairo, though in these days of waning faith comparatively insignificant, is said formerly to have numbered a hundred thousand. I was assured at Akaba that the famous Sheikh Hussein, chief of the Aloween, possessed not less than eight thousand; but though the wants of the pilgrims at the annual visit to Mecca, when the services of this eminent personage are in "honorable request," must furnish employment for a great number of these animals, I cannot but suspect that this estimate is much too liberal. How a caravan of one hundred thousand camels could find pasturage in any part of the Arabian desert it is not easy to comprehend; and we can hardly suppose that, on leaving Cairo, the pilgrims carried with them a stock of provender for forty-five days, even making all due allowance for the supplies provided by the public authorities and private speculators at the various stations on the route.

The vast armies of half-civilized nations in ancient times, and of the crusaders in the middle ages, that made long campaigns through barren or deserted countries, without any commissariat or other known source of supply, indeed make the Arab accounts of great caravans more credible, if not quite explicable; but after all, something must doubtless be allowed for the Oriental propensity to deal very loosely with numbers and quantities. This habit renders it a matter of extreme difficulty to collect reliable statistical information in Eastern countries. In fact, although with us the Arabic *numerals* have become a symbol of certainty, yet a traveller among Orientals, and especially the Bedouins, soon finds, that nothing is so uncertain as Arabic *numbers*. I attempted in Egypt to ascertain from the most intelligent native sources, the *average* annual produce of the date palm. The reader will judge of the value of my statistics on this point, when he is told that the estimates of experienced and apparently intelligent persons varied from fifty or sixty to seven hundred pounds. At Mount Sinai, you are told that the rugged staircase by which you climb Jabel Moosa, consists of fifteen thousand steps, and many European travellers have repeated this foolish story, without stopping to consider that as the difference of level between the convent and the peak is scarcely two thousand feet, the rise of the steps would be but an inch and a half. The rooms in the great Armenian convent at Jerusalem are popularly stated at fifteen thousand, certainly fifty times the true number. Every day's experience in the East will furnish the traveller with similar instances of absurd exaggeration. It is partly, perhaps, to the characteristic vagueness of perception among the Orientals, and the want of familiarity with numerical combinations, that we are to ascribe this uncertainty. Besides, there are scarcely any authorized and exact standards of value, weight, or measure, and the habits of Eastern life in general present less frequent occasion for precise estimation than in European countries. It is, therefore, quite natural that the people should have very loose notions of relative magnitudes, and should accordingly use numbers much at random. The pride of an Oriental seldom permits him to admit ignorance. He will always lie or guess rather than avow inability to answer any question, and his error is very sure to lie in the way of multiplication. But after all these allowances are made, it will still be found that an innate and habitual disregard of the truth is eminently characteristic of the Oriental mind, Christian and pagan alike, and one must have known the Levant to be able to conceive how readily persons intelligent and otherwise respectable will prefer a lie to the truth, when the slightest advantage is to be gained by the use of a falsehood.

# CHAPTER XVI.

## GEOGRAPHICAL RANGE OF THE CAMEL.

THE camel, as we have already seen, exists and thrives through a wide range of climates, and under a great variety of conditions. It does not appear that any temperature is too high for the one-humped species. Southern Arabia, where he is found in great perfection, is one of the hottest countries on the globe, and the only obstacle to his diffusion through the whole extent of the equatorial regions, is the dampness of many tropical climates. He seems entirely indifferent to the fiercest heats of an African sun. I have often watched his habits in this respect in the desert, and though we sometimes encamped near palms and other trees, or where he could readily have found a shelter in the cool shadow of a rock, I could never discover that, even under the most glaring light and scorching heat, he at all preferred the shade to the sun.

But in these same climates, he is exposed to a very considerable degree of cold. The nocturnal radiation under the clear sky of the Libyan desert often reduces the temperature to the freezing point. In latitude 25° N., Lyon saw the thermometer fall to 26°. The mercury was below 32° several mornings in succession, ice formed half an inch in thickness, and the water-skins were frozen. In the autumn of 1850, it was so cold between Korasko and Khartum on the Nile, that caravans were unable to move for two or three days; Denham and Clapperton experienced hard frosts in latitude 13° N., but we do not learn that the camels of the country were in any of these instances seriously injured by this severe weather. Other breeds of the same species support far greater degrees of cold without much apparent suffering. The one-humped camel abounds in conjunction with the Bactrian throughout the immediate basin of the Caspian and the Sea of Azoff, and far to the east under the same parallel. In this latitude the winters are of great severity, and according to Fraser, travellers sometimes perish of cold even in the vicinity of Teheran. The Calmucks, who possess great numbers of both species, spend their summers in higher latitudes, migrate in autumn to the south of 50° N. L.,[1] and pass the winter on

[1] This migration finds its counterpart in central Africa, where the camel moves northwards from the highlands to

the lower Volga and the steppes near the Caspian, where there is an abundance of reeds and rushes to serve as fodder for their cattle during the cold season.

Beyond the steppes inhabited by the Calmucks, the Arabian camel is succeeded exclusively by the Bactrian,[1] and some of the septs of that tribe, as for example those with whom Bergmann sojourned and wandered, possess only the latter species. It is only in the coldest climates inhabited by the Bactrian, that he requires any protection against the rigors of winter. Georgi states that, in the vicinity of Lake Baikal, the camel is sewed up in coarse woollen cloth during the extremest cold, but even here he receives no fodder from his master, but is left to shift for himself by browsing on the twigs of the birch, the wild plum, the Siberian pine, and the few shrubs that peep out through the snows. On the plains of the Irtysch he thrives extremely well, in spite of the piercing

the Sahara on the approach of the rainy season, with the swarms of insects that accompany that period.

1 Although the Bactrian, as has been before observed, is not bred in Arabia or in Africa, he is nevertheless known to Arabic literature. Baron Hammer-Purgstall quotes from an Arabic poem this couplet: —

> Joints of the Bactrian did his table boast,
> Choice fare and drink betrayed the generous host.

cold, and is strong enough to carry from three to five riders. They are sewed up in felt cloths, and large felts are stretched between the huts of their masters, under which they gather for shelter. Pallas observed the same custom among the Calmucks, but Bergmann, who lived some time among that people, says the felts are not required for their protection against the cold, but that they are merely a sort of housing for the pack-saddle, which is used the whole year through. They are less injuriously affected by the severest winters, he observes, than the horse, the ox, or the sheep, and they bear hunger and thirst almost as well as the Arabian. Erman[1] says, under date of February 20, and with a temperature of 25° of Fahrenheit below zero, "On the Chinese side, (at Kiachta,) we saw seventy fine camels turned loose and feeding on the frozen and withered grass. They fear the severe winters of this climate as little as the parching heat in the sand-steppes. The alternation of thaw and frost alone is dangerous to them. The sharp and brittle icy crust, which forms under such circumstances upon the surface of the snow, wounds their legs and feet, as is elsewhere observed to be the case with the stag and the roe."

[1] Reisen, II. 154.

So numerous is the camel in these frozen realms, that almost the whole commerce between Russia and China, by way of Kiachta, is carried on by means of them; and they transport merchandise over the vast distance between Orenburg on the Ural, and Petropawlowsk on the peninsula of Kamtschatka. In the month of October, Timkovski met on the desert of Gobi, in latitude 46°, and at the height of 2,500 feet above the sea, a herd of 20,000 camels; the Russian expedition against Khiva and Bokhara, in 1840, employed more than an equal number; and Berghaus estimates the number of camels in European Russia at not less than 100,000.

Father Huc's lively narrative of his travels in Tartary is full of similar proofs of the power of the Bactrian to brave the icy frosts and chilling blasts of that frigid region, and we may reasonably conclude that the camel is able to endure the greatest extremes of temperature known in climates habitable by civilized man.

The range of countries through which the camel is spread, has been greatly extended within the historical period, and even within comparatively recent times. I have already alluded to the fact of his late introduction into the African continent, where, although he cannot be said to have been unknown, he certainly did not come into general use earlier than the third or fourth century of the Christian era. The Asiatic Goths who made an irruption into the valleys of the Dniester and Danube towards the end of the fourth century, appear to have brought both the Bactrian and the Arabian in their train, as both are represented among the spoil of the Goths on the triumphal column erected by Arcadius at Constantinople, in honor of the victory over that people won by his father Theodosius, in the year 386. From the northern shores of the Black Sea they spread very gradually northwards until, having reached the zone inhabited by the reindeer, they appear to have met their natural limit in this direction. They were introduced into Granada by the Moors in the middle ages, and are still used in that country. The Norman conquerors carried them to the Canary Islands in the fifteenth century, and the Turks to Cyprus somewhat later. An unsuccessful attempt was made to naturalize them in Peru in the sixteenth century, and with better success in Venezuela, where Humboldt found them at the beginning of the present century. At what period they were carried to Tuscany is matter of dispute, but they have bred there at least two hundred years, and it is remarkable that they were not introduced into the Persian provinces bordering on the Caspian, until the construction of roads through that region by Shah Abbas, about the time of the first colonization of our eastern States.[1]

His progress eastward from the two centres where the Bactrian and the Arabian appear to have respectively originated—the desert of Gobi and the greater Arabian peninsula—has been equally gradual, and it is only within the present century that he has been introduced, though not with encouraging success, into the damp climate and tropical luxuriance of the islands of the Indian Ocean.

That he will continue to spread, until he finds a home in all thinly populated countries with tropical or temperate climates, and such conditions of soil as occur in his original birthplaces, there can be little doubt, and we may therefore confidently expect his naturalization in South Africa, Australia, the desert of Atacama, Southern Chili and Buenos Ayres, and our own New Mexican and Californian territories.

1 Hanway and some other travellers have ascribed the former rarity of the camel in the southern basin of the Caspian to the abundance of boxwood, upon the foliage of which the animal greedily feeds, but which seldom fails to prove fatal to him. Later observation has not confirmed this opinion, nor is it known that any plant which he inclines to eat is injurious to him.

# CHAPTER XVII.

## INTRODUCTION OF THE CAMEL INTO THE UNITED STATES.

THE question of the practicability and advantages of introducing the camel into the United States is a topic of much interest and importance.

Among those who are practically familiar with the habits and properties of the camel, and who have studied the physical conditions of our territory west of the Mississippi, there is, I believe, little or no difference of opinion on the subject; and I am persuaded that the ultimate success of judicious and persevering effort is certain, and will be attended with important advantages. At the same time, it must not be concealed that, as much depends on a point that nothing but experience can determine, — the selection, namely, of the particular breeds best adapted to our climate, soil, and other local conditions, — the result of a first experiment is extremely uncertain.

The question must be considered under two aspects: the one regarding the camel as simply a beast of burden; the other, his value as an animal of war. But even if it is conceded, which I by no means admit, that the organization of a proper mounted dromedary corps is impracticable or inexpedient, it does not, by any means, follow that the camel may not be of great value in the commissariat, and in all that belongs to the mere movement of bodies of men, as well as in the independent transportation of military stores and all the munitions of war.

The first point to be discussed is the adaptation of any variety of either species to the climate and soil of any portion of our territory. So far as mere extremes of temperature are concerned, it is quite certain that we have nowhere, west of the Mississippi, fiercer or more long-continued heats, more parched deserts, or wastes more destitute of vegetation, than those of the regions where the Arabian camel is found in his highest perfection; and the Bactrian thrives in climates as severe as even the coldest portion of our northeastern territory.

There is, however, it must be admitted, one point of difference between our general climate and that of the eastern continent, which has an unfavorable bearing on the question. I refer to the greater moisture of our atmosphere and the greater frequency of rains during the summer season. In general, the countries where the camel thrives have a proper dry season, little or no rain falling during the summer months. But to this rule there are exceptions. The valley of the lower Danube has summer rains, and a very wet autumn, winter, and spring; and many northern Asiatic districts are subject to similar climatic conditions. But the objection, whatever may be its force, seems to apply merely to the proportion of the year during which the animal can labor, and not to its influence upon his constitution; because, it appears that in the cold and damp Russian provinces, the camel is less subject to disease, and attains a greater longevity, than in any other part of the world; and it is remarkable that in the Crimea, he is little used in the hottest and driest season, because the heat is found too great for that variety, and his services are most valuable in winter.

But there are important exceptions to the general moist character of the North American climate, and these occur precisely in the latitudes where the soil and natural productions are best suited to the habits and wants of the camel, and where at the same time his peculiar properties could be best made available for the service of man.

The driest and most barren portions of our territory are,

I. The Great Plain which forms the eastern

slope of the Rocky Mountains. This district embraces nearly the entire valley of the Rio Grande, and extends northwards beyond the northern boundary of the United States. Its eastern border runs upon the longitude of about 96° W. from the Rio Grande to the parallel of 37°, where it inclines to the northeast, and in latitude 44° meets the meridian of 92° W. It now turns to the northwest, and crosses our northern boundary on the meridian of 94° W.; westwardly, it is bounded by the Rocky Mountains. Throughout this vast space, whose area is considerably greater than that of all the American States east of the Alleghanies, the total annual precipitation, according to Blodget's Kyetal Charts, nowhere exceeds twenty five inches, and this quantity is confined to its eastern border, with the exception of a narrow belt between the parallels of 35° and 37°. The central portion northward of this belt has but fifteen inches of rain and snow, the residue twenty inches annually. In the lower valley of the Rio Grande, the precipitation is twenty inches, more to the northwest from ten to fifteen only.

II. The Great Basin of the Interior. The southern division of this basin lies between the parallels of 30° and 40° N. and the meridians of 110° and 120° W. In a small part of the eastern portion of this division, the rain and snow amount to twenty inches, elsewhere the precipitation is from three to five, and in some localities ten inches, for the year. In the northern division the precipitation is ten inches for the centre, twenty for the borders.

In the eastern basin the winter is the driest season, the summer in the western, and the quantity of rain and snow appears, throughout the whole extent of both, to be too small to interfere seriously with the utility, or prejudice the health, of the camel.

Large tracts in both basins are deserts, not indeed absolutely destitute of vegetation, but yielding neither grass nor shrubbery suited to the support of any quadruped but the camel, though there seems to be good cause to believe that this animal, in reasonable numbers, would find sufficient and appropriate pasturage. The deserts in their general character bear a considerable resemblance to those of Arabia, but the deposits of sand appear to be less extensive than the corresponding formations in the Libyan desert. Water is only met with at long intervals, and the rivers sometimes run at the bottom of ravines so deep and with walls so precipitous, that their beds are quite inaccessible from the plateau above. There is, however, no evidence of the existence of any American desert, where water cannot be obtained as often as the animal economy of the camel requires it. None of the passes of the Rocky Mountains are more rugged or steeper than those of Arabia or Tartary, and there is every probability, that all the known routes between the Mississippi and the Pacific coast, would prove entirely practicable to either species of the camel.

On alluvial and other soft soils, caravans using the camel will no doubt be obliged to halt during rains and until the ground is dry; but this is no more than the emigrant wagon-trains across the plains are compelled to do under similar circumstances; and upon all other surfaces, one or the other of the species may be used without regard to weather or to season.

So far, then, as climate and soil are concerned, it may be regarded as quite certain that the Bactrian camel can sustain any exposure to which he would be subjected in our trans-Mississippian territory; and there is no reason to doubt that the mezquit-acacia, and other shrubs, and the saline plants known to exist in many of those regions, would furnish him an appropriate and acceptable nutriment.

It is not impossible that some of our desert plants attractive to the palate of the camel may prove injurious to him; but in this event, that mysterious law of nature, whereby even animal instincts accommodate themselves to new conditions, will soon teach him to avoid them. It is observed in the sheep-growing states of New England, that sheep, brought from localities where the laurel (Kalmia) is unknown, to those where it abounds, often feed upon its foliage and are poisoned by it, while those which are bred in pastures half-covered by this shrub very seldom touch it.

I cannot speak with equal confidence of the ability of the Arabian camel, and especially of the mahari of the desert, to bear corresponding trials. All high-bred animals are delicate, and impatient of exposure to great extremes and sudden changes; and although Denham and Clapperton speak of hard frosts in latitude 13° north, and Lyon records a temperature four degrees below the freezing-point, in districts constantly traversed by the mahari, yet the finest and fleetest animals will not bear the winter climate of Algiers.[1] But although we may not be able to breed dromedaries of a speed equal to the most extraordinary performances I have described, there is no reason to doubt that the more common animal, which will travel eight or ten hours a day at five miles an hour, for many days in succession, and with greater speed for a shorter period, can be bred and used with ad-

[1] Carbuccia, p. 3.

vantage throughout our southwestern territories, and on all the more southern passes of the mountains which divide the valley of the Mississippi from the Pacific slope, as well as throughout the State of California.

# CHAPTER XVIII.

## MILITARY USES OF THE CAMEL.

THE ancient Asiatics, and, at a later period, the Romans, made a very extensive use of the dromedary in war, not only for the transportation of men and munitions, but as technical cavalry in actual combat.

Herodotus, Xenophon, Livy, Pliny the elder, Diodorus, Herodian, Procopius, and other ancient authors, speak of the military uses of the camel, in terms which show that he was employed in war to an extent only inferior to the horse; and it does not appear that there is anything in his constitution or habits which in any degree unfits him for rendering essential service in modern warfare. The Bactrian is still employed in Persia, Bokhara, and Tartary, for military purposes, and especially for the conveyance of light pieces of artillery, which are mounted between the humps, and used in that position, the camel kneeling while the gun is loaded, aimed, and fired. Burckhardt saw the

Arabian used in the same way, in Syria, the gun being mounted on the pack-saddle. In modern European armies they have hardly been employed, except by Napoleon, in transporting the baggage of his army in the Syrian campaign, and in his celebrated dromedary regiment in Egypt; and, more recently, by the army of occupation in Algeria. Upon the march from Egypt to Syria, the baggage, the camp equipage, and the sick, of an army of fifteen thousand men, were transported solely by camels.

In the campaigns of Mehemet Ali and Ibrahim Pacha, against the Wahabis, in Arabia, camels were the only means of transportation for heavy ordnance, and every description of military material, required for the large army of the Pacha; and though great numbers of them perished from the fatigues and privations of the march, yet the loss from this cause was less than it would have been had any other means of conveyance been resorted to.

It is remarkable that the military archives of France furnish little or no information, beyond the mere number of the corps, respecting the dromedary regiment of the army of Egypt, the historical documents belonging to the subject having been chiefly lost or suppressed; and all we know concerning it is derived from an imperfect and erroneous account in the great work on Egypt, and a late paper by Jomard, one of the savans who accompanied the expedition. Without entering into minute detail, it must suffice to say that this regiment, which numbered something less than five hundred men, was organized in the main like a regiment of cavalry, and performed the same general service, with the most brilliant success. Although the men were taken from the infantry, a very short time was required to teach them the new discipline and drill, and the animals were habituated to the necessary evolutions in an incredibly short space of time. The services rendered by the corps were of a most important character, and its performances, according to Prétot, were quite unprecedented in military annals.

I abstain from particulars with reference to the services of this regiment, because the evidence on which they rest is not entirely conclusive; but there is no doubt that Napoleon himself, and all the military authorities of the time, considered them to have been of great value.

The recent experiments in Algeria, have proved altogether satisfactory to the officers charged with them, and their reports seem decisive with respect to the utility of the camel as an animal of war, though the apparent results have certainly not been so brilliant as they are alleged to have been in the case of the dromedary regiment in Egypt.

The prejudices of the officers and men against the use of this awkward and ungraceful animal in the regular service, have proved very difficult to overcome. The peculiar organization of the French commissariat has interposed serious pecuniary obstacles, and the government has always seemed disinclined to consider the question in a spirit of liberality and candor. It is, however, proved that the use of the dromedary contributes in a most important degree to the economy, the celerity, and the efficiency of military movements in desert regions; and I cannot doubt that it would prove a powerful auxiliary in all measures tending to keep in check the hostile Indians on the frontier, as well as in maintaining the military and postal communication between our Pacific territory and the east.

There are few more imposing spectacles than a body of armed men, advancing under the quick pace of the trained dromedary; and this sight, with the ability of the animal to climb ascents impracticable to horses, and thus to transport mountain howitzers, light artillery, stores, and other military material into the heart of the mountains, would strike with a salutary terror the Comanches, Lipans, and other savage tribes upon our borders.

The habits of these Indians much resemble those of the nomade Arabs, and the introduction of the camel among them would modify their modes of life as much as the use of the horse has done. For a time, indeed, the possession of this animal would only increase their powers of mischief; but it might, in the long run, prove the means of raising them to that state of semi-civilized life, of which alone their native wastes seem susceptible. The products of the camel, milk, wool, skin, and flesh, would prove of inestimable value to these tribes, which otherwise are likely soon to perish with the buffalo and other large game animals; and the profit of transportation across our inland desert, might have the same effect in reclaiming these barbarians, which it has had upon the Arabs of the Sinaïtic peninsula.

Among the advantages of the camel for military purposes, may be mentioned the economy of his original cost, as compared with the horse or mule, when once introduced and fairly domesticated;[1] the simplicity and cheapness of his saddle and other furniture, which every

[1] The price of the camel is exceedingly low in all countries where he is bred. Except for the highest breed, maharis, it nowhere, except in the Crimea, exceeds fifty dollars, and is in general considerably below this sum. The reason of this is that it costs nothing to breed the animal. The dam

soldier can manufacture for himself; the exemption from the trouble and expense of providing for his sustenance, and from dressing, sheltering, or shoeing him; his great docility, his general freedom from disease, his longevity, the magnitude of his burden, and the great celerity of his movements, his extraordinary fearlessness,[1] the safety of his rider, whether from falls or the viciousness of the animal, the economical value of his flesh, and the applicability of his hair and his skin to many purposes of military use or convenience, the resources which in extreme cases the milk might furnish, and finally his great powers of abstinence from both food and drink.[2]

A point which deserves to be mentioned is the comparatively insignificant loss involved in the

continues to labor during the whole period of gestation, (which runs according to climate, from eleven, or in some cases, ten to twelve months,) and even the dropping of a foal scarcely delays her march. Denham and Clapperton, I. c. 3; Ritter, XIII. 610. The young requires no care and little training, and is already serviceable in his third year.

1 Carbuccia, p. 34, p. 168.

2 The use of the camel has enabled the corps which have employed it in Algeria, to dispense altogether with a baggage train, as the animal can transport a very considerable burden, in addition to the soldier and his accoutrements, at a much more rapid rate than the ordinary march of a column of infantry or artillery.

death of a camel belonging to the baggage train. The loss of a single horse or mule may not only occasion the abandonment of the load, but of the wagon, often an expensive vehicle, to which he was attached; whereas, in case of the death of a burden camel, the only equipage lost is his pack-saddle, which is of very trifling pecuniary value. Wheel carriages and harnesses are exposed to constant breakage in crossing the plains. The means of repairing them are not always at hand, and even when much time has been spent in putting them to rights, they not unfrequently break down altogether before the journey is half completed. The employment of the burden camel is attended with none of these risks and inconveniences.

I may add another advantage, which will be appreciated by all who know the difficulty of conducting a caravan of mules or horses across the plains. I refer to the security from stampedes and other nocturnal alarms and losses. The dromedary is a much less timid animal than the horse or mule, and he is not sufficiently gregarious in his habits to be readily influenced by a panic terror. The mode by which he is confined at night, furnishes a complete security against escapes from fright or other causes. As he lies down, he folds the forelegs under the body. The Arab passes a loop around one or both of the folded limbs, above the knee, and secures the end of the cord around the neck. When both legs are thus shackled, the camel can rise only to the knee; if one only is hoppled, he rises with difficulty, and moves very slowly; and if an Indian were to cut the loop, and thus free the animal, and even succeed in mounting him, he would not be able, without a previous practice, which he has not the means of acquiring, to put him up to such a speed as to elude pursuit.

There is another point which I have never heard insisted on, but which has often struck me with some force in riding the camel. I mean the greater range of vision which, in a level country, the greater elevation of the seat gives the rider. The eye of the horseman is upon an average scarcely eight feet above the ground. Upon the dromedary it is two feet higher, and commands a wider range accordingly.

To all these advantages there are, so far as I am aware, but few drawbacks. The whole question has been much discussed among the military men of France, with reference to the employment of the camel in Algeria, and the examination of the various points presented in these discussions forms the most valuable part of Carbuccia's work. He reviews the various objections, which have been urged against the introduction of the camel into the military service, and I think disposes of them all satisfactorily. I do not discover any local objections growing out of peculiarities of our soil, climate, habits, or institutions; and, on the other hand, the different character and circumstances of the hostile Indians, who are without, and could not procure the animal, form a new argument in favor of the project. Another argument upon the same side is the fact that the distances over which he would be used are far greater, and the country to be traversed more inadequately supplied with the necessaries required to satisfy the wants of other animals of transport, than is the case in the territory where the camel has operated in Algeria.

The expense of a full and fair trial would be a sum very insignificant in comparison with the probable results. The experiment now trying under the small appropriation made at the last session of congress, if successful, is of course decisive, but if not, it is to be hoped that it may be repeated on a larger scale, and with a greater variety of animals.

An objection which ought to be noticed is the difficulty of accustoming horses and other domestic animals to the sight of the camel. The objection is as old as Herodotus and Xenophon, and Pliny supposes that this animal has a natural antipathy to the horse. In most countries where they are bred together, one hears of no difficulty on this score; but it is said that the fears of the one animal or the antipathies of the other have been found an inconvenience in Tuscany; and even in Tartary, where the Bactrian has been long in use, it appears from Father Huc, that horses regard them with fear or dislike; but the objection is of no great force as applied to the sparsely populated regions of the far West, and as the multiplication of the animal would be gradual and slow, it is not likely that any great or general evil would flow from this source.

The most serious inconvenience which would attend the use of the camel in marching through a country inhabited by hostile Indians, is the necessity of allowing him to wander in search of food; but as he habitually returns to camp before sunset, of his own accord, and never feeds, and very seldom stirs during the night, he would require to be watched only for a couple of hours during the whole twenty-four.

The testimony is so strong in favor of the Bactrian for northern latitudes, and of the cross between the two species for the general purposes of a burden animal, that it is highly important to import a sufficient number of the former species to test the qualities of both the pure breed and the hybrid, with reference to our own special wants. Now that peace is restored, the Bactrian might readily be obtained from the Russo-European provinces on the Black Sea, but as the camels of those provinces are trained only for draught, it would be more advisable to procure them from the Calmucks, in the neighborhood of the Caspian, where they are used for burden and for the saddle, and, according to Bergmann, possess great speed, and they could be shipped at some of the ports of the sea of Azow, or they might perhaps, with even greater convenience, be bought at Petropawlowsk, on the Pacific, at the season of the visit of the caravans, and landed in California.

The best and fleetest dromedaries are those of Nubia, and of Yemen in Arabia, but the latter are greatly inferior in both size and strength to those of Nubia, as well as to the mahari of the Sahara. That either of these breeds would thrive in any part of our territory is hardly probable, and there does not seem to exist any present strong motive for attempting on a large scale their naturalization in the United States.

In the introduction of the animal, advantage will no doubt be taken of the experience acquired by the French in Algeria, and it may be reasonably hoped that European and American intelligence will more fully develop the powers of the camel, and thus add a new and important resource to the means and agencies of Christian civilization.

"If," says General Marey Monge, "cavalry had been unknown in France, and we, seeing the great advantages derived from it by the

Arabs, had now for the first time attempted to introduce it into our military service, we should have had a thousand difficulties to overcome. Objections would have been made on the score of kicks and bites, errors would have been committed in the choice of saddles and bridles, the horses would have met with accidents, or contracted ailments from our want of experience and ignorance of farriery; in the first engagements, our mounted men would have been thrown or run away with, they would have been clumsy in managing their arms on horseback, and probably been roughly handled by the superior skill of the Arab horsemen. A party would have been formed against the innovators, who would themselves have become disgusted, and the attempt to introduce mounted corps would perhaps have been abandoned; but if, in spite of accidents, mistakes, and losses, we had persevered, we should have ended by forming what we have now, an efficient and excellent cavalry."

This argument is as valid with us as it was in Algeria; and if the experiment shall be tried in the United States without success, it will probably fail for reasons as specious but as inconclusive as those which General Monge supposes against the introduction of cavalry into the French military service.

# APPENDIX.

# APPENDIX A.

## Notes from Baron Hammer-Purgstall's Paper Das Kamel, in the Denkschriften der Kaiserlichen Akademie der Wissenschaften. *Phil. Hist.* ; Classe VI.

Baron Hammer's paper is founded wholly on oriental, and chiefly on lexicographical and poetical authorities, and gives therefore rather the philological and imaginative than the descriptive and historical view of the subject. None of the numerous *special* Arabic works on the camel, whose authors or titles are referred to by Hammer, are found in any library in Europe ; but he seems to have collected from lexicons, from the wide range of Arabic poetry, and from other sources, all the passages of Arabic literature, which throw light on the relatives of this animal to Arab life.

Although, therefore, it cannot be said that many new facts of physiological interest are brought to light by the portion of the Essay now published, it is highly probable, that the original texts which are to follow, and which, as Hammer says, " contain much that is new to the naturalist," will, to use his own language, " show how natural history and physiology may be advanced by philology and the knowledge of words."

The paper is divided into four principal sections,

the *first* treating generally of the camel and his animal life, the *second* of the members, constituents, and products of his body, his properties and qualities, and the *third* of his conditions, uses, and treatment. These sections are subdivided into sixteen chapters. The *fourth* section, in four chapters, gives the few passages of the Koran in which mention is made of the camel; the traditional expressions of Mohammed referring to the animal; one hundred and forty-seven proverbs and proverbial phrases; and numerous passages translated from twenty Arabic poets, descriptive or illustrative of the habits, uses, and value of the camel.

As might be expected, many of these chapters add nothing to the existing stock of information on the subject, though frequently interesting from the glimpses they afford of oriental life and oriental character.

I confine my excerpts to passages which supply omissions in the foregoing pages.

Chap. I. Names of the camel. The general name of the animal is not, as is mistakenly supposed, the Arabic word dscheml, or dschemel, (jĕml, in English orthography,) but Ibl Dscheml is only used of the *male*, nâket, (written naga by most travellers) of the *female*, when there is occasion to specify the sex. All the other numerous names of the camel indicate age, sex, or properties, and Ibl is the only word which expresses the species in the abstract, without reference to accidents.

Chap. II. A small delicate and pointed ear is a sign of "blood," and the ear of high-bred animals is often cut, so that a strip of the lobe hangs pendent. In a note to this chapter, the author observes that *el-Bochti*, the proper specific designation of the Bactrian, is sometimes applied to *strong* camels generally.

CHAP. IV. The camel does not attain his full strength and perfection until the age of nine years, and his utmost term of life, like that of man, is fourscore.

CHAP. VIII. When the foal is to be weaned, he is turned towards Canopus, at its rising, his master gives him a blow on the ear, and says, with an oath, "hereafter drinkest thou no drop of milk!" Hence the newly-weaned camel is called *Lathim*, the ear-boxed.

CHAP. IX. For want of vegetable nutriment, the camel is sometimes fed with fat and flesh, but this diet weakens and enervates him. *Katád*, a species of tragacanth, and *Thiláh*, a thorny acacia, are said to produce colic.

CHAP. X. Different animals require water at different intervals, from one day to ten, and are named accordingly.

CHAP. XI. The eyes are protected against the cold by *blinders*, not unlike those worn by European horses. The Arab judges whether the animal is fat enough for slaughter by looking at the eye.

CHAP. XIII. White is the favorite color, next black. There are special names for those spotted or mottled with white or black, as well as for other colors.

CHAP. XV. The milk of the camel is intoxicating. Various extracts are given, showing the use of the animal as a beast of the saddle in battle.

CHAP. XVI. p. 91 mentions the protection of young camels against cold by blankets or housings.

# APPENDIX B.

## SIR EVERARD HOME'S ANATOMY OF THE STOMACH.

"The camel's stomach anteriorly forms one large bag, but when laid open this is found to be divided into two compartments on its posterior part, by a strong ridge, which passes down from the right side of the orifice of the œsophagus in a longitudinal direction. This ridge forms one side of a groove that leads to the orifice of the second cavity, and is continued on beyond that part, becoming one boundary to the cellular structure met with in that situation. From this ridge eight strong muscular bands go off at right angles, and afterwards form curved lines till they are insensibly lost in the coats of the stomach. These are at equal distances from each other, and, being intersected in a regular way by transverse septa, form the cells. This cellular structure is in the left compartment of the first cavity, and there is another of a more superficial kind on the right, placed in exactly the opposite direction, made up of twenty-one rows of smaller cells, but entirely unconnected with the great ridge. On the left side of the termination of the œsophagus, a broad muscular band has its origin from the coats of the first cavity, and passes down in the form of a fold parallel to the great ridge, till it enters the orifice of the second, where it takes another direction. It is continued along the upper edge of that cavity, and terminates within the orifice of a small bag, which may be termed the third cavity. This band on one side and the great ridge on the other form a canal, which leads from the œsophagus down to the cellular structure in the lower part of the first cavity. The orifice of the second cavity, when this muscle is not in action, is nearly shut; it is at right angles to the side of the first. The second cavity forms a pendulous bag, in which there are twelve rows of cells formed by as many muscular bands, passing in a transverse direction, and intersected by weaker muscular bands, so as to form the orifice of the cells. Above these cells, between them and the muscle which passes along the upper part of this cavity, is a smooth surface, extending from the orifice of this cavity to the termination in the third.

"From this account, it is evident that the second cavity neither receives the solid food in the first instance, as in the bullock, nor does the food afterwards pass into the cavity or cellular structure. The food first passes into the first compartment of the first cavity, and that portion of it which lies in the recess immediately below the entrance of the œsophagus, under which the cells are situated, is kept moist, and is readily returned into the mouth along the groove formed for that purpose, by the action of the strong muscle which surrounds this part of the stomach, so that the cellular portion of the first cavity in the camel performs the same office as the second in ruminants with horns. While the camel is drinking, the action of the muscular band opens the orifice of the second cavity at the same time that it directs the water into it; and when the cells of that cavity are full, the rest runs off into the cellular structure of the first cavity immediately below, and afterwards into the general cavity. It would appear that camels when accustomed to go journeys, in which they are kept for an unusual number of days without water, acquire the power of dilating the cells so as to make them contain a more than ordinary quantity as a supply for their journey; at least, such is the account given by those who have been in Egypt. When the cud has been chewed, it has to pass along the upper part of the second cavity before it can reach the third. How this is effected without its falling into the cellular portion, could not, from any inspection of dried specimens, be ascertained; but when the recent stomach is accurately examined, the mode in which this is managed becomes very obvious. At the time that the cud has to pass from the mouth, the muscular band contracts with so much force that it not only opens the orifice of the second cavity, but acting on the mouth of the third brings it forward into the second, by which means the muscular ridges that separate the rows of cells are brought close together, so as to exclude these cavities from the canal though which the cud passes.

"It appears that the small cavity regarded by Daubenton as analogous to a reticulum, was not considered by Mr. John Hunter as of sufficient importance to be ranked as a distinct stomach; and the water-bag must therefore, in his opinion, have held the place of the honey-comb bag in the horned ruminants. And when we compare the relation of the reticulum to the rumen in that tribe with the corresponding free communication which subsists between the water-bag and rumen in the camel tribe; and when also we observe in both the precise correspondence in the mode of communication of these two cavities with the œsophagus, and with the muscular apparatus destined to convey the remasticated food beyond their apertures into the third cavity, and at the same time find an approach to the peculiar disposition of the cells of the water-bag in the reticulum of some of the horned ruminants, it becomes evident that the two cavities are analogous, the reticulum of the camels being modified for its destined function by the greater development of the secondary cells, by the absence of a cuticular lining, and by the production of the inner layer of the muscular tunic, which forms the apparatus for closing the orifice of the primary cells. The third cavity, therefore, which could not have been recognized as a distinct compartment in the llama, and which undoubtedly receives the remasticated food in the camel, ought rather to be regarded as a peculiar structure, to which nothing analogous is to be found in the stomachs of the horned ruminants."

# APPENDIX C.

## NOTE ON THE BACTRIAN CAMEL.

I SUBJOIN, in a connected and condensed form, the substance of replies to queries which I addressed to correspondents in the southern provinces of Russia respecting the Bactrian camel.

But a single species of camel, namely, the Bactrian or two-humped animal, is known in Southern Russia. The average height from the top of the head to the sole of the foot is about four arschin (nine feet four inches) in Bessarabia. In the Crimea his height is stated at about seven feet.[1] He weighs about one third more than the ox, which is here estimated at nine hundred pounds. In the former province, the mean duration of his life is estimated at thirty-five years, in the latter at from sixty to seventy-five, and in some cases it is said to extend to a century.[2]

[1] The expression *about* four arschin is probably not to be taken very literally, as it indicates a considerably higher stature than is generally ascribed to any breed of the animal, except, in rare cases, to the mahari of the Sahara. It does not appear from my memoranda, whether the measurement in the Crimea was from the shoulders or the hump.

[2] If this remarkable difference between the Bessarabian and the Crimean camel really exists, may it not be ascribed to the drier summers of the latter province, the more desert character of the soil, and the freer range allowed to the animal?

From the beginning of the fifth year he is used for riding and draught in Bessarabia; from the beginning of the fourth, in the Crimea, but for draught alone. The female produces her first foal after the fifth year, and thereafter every second year. The time of gestation is a year, that of lactation two years, and the dam is used during the latter period.

In the Crimea, the camel is used only for drawing heavy loads, but not for ploughing or other agricultural labor, on account of his "unsteadiness." In Bessarabia, however, he is employed regularly for all the labors of rural industry.

His fleece weighs about ten pounds, and is shed in the summer, if not plucked off by hand. The Tartars manufacture a coarse cloth from it. The wool sells at five silver rubles the pood of about thirty six pounds Eng. The skin is thought not equal to that of the ox. It is principally used raw for thongs, ropes, straps, &c., and sells for three or four silver rubles. The milk is used in a great variety of ways. The yield is about two quarts. The flesh is eaten and resembles beef, if the animal is fat, otherwise it is tough and disagreeable. The bones and intestines have not been applied to any practical use.

The Bactrian travels from seventy to seventy-five *versts* (46 to 50 miles) a day, without eating, drinking, or halting. His gait is regular, and his speed considerably exceeds that of the ox. He cannot be used on muddy ground, not so much from any liability to slip and fall, as because the wet earth adheres to his feet, and makes him restive and impatient. In the Crimea he is principally employed in the winter. His feet require no shoeing or other protection, and he travels perfectly well on snow, ice, and frozen ground. Although he labors the whole year through in Bessarabia, he is of comparatively little use in the summer in the Crimea, where he is only employed for draught. At that season, if yoked to the wagon, he is annoyed by the heat, sweats profusely and becomes exhausted. His feet do not suffer from travelling on soils impregnated with mineral salts.

His gait, which is an amble, is by no means wearisome to the rider, and he never stumbles in going up hill or down. He is in general docile, obedient, and patient, but in the rutting season, the male is ill tempered and sometimes dangerous. Two or four camels are harnessed to wagons and sledges with a yoke resembling an ox yoke and are guided by the halter. Upon a dry road, a pair will draw from eighty to one hundred poods, (twenty-nine to thirty-seven hundred pounds.) He is never harnessed singly.

He goes twice as long as the horse without drinking, and is content with the poorest fodder. In the summer, he feeds on thistles, weeds, rushes, reeds, and in general on coarse vegetables, which are not eaten by other animals, and in fact, he scarcely rejects any green thing. In winter, his nutriment consists of hay, straw, and coarse fodder. He requires from fifty to seventy pounds of dry food per day, but it is found good economy to feed him well, as he performs much more service, than if poorly nourished.

When he is in good case, the humps, of which the

forward one is perhaps a little the largest, are erect, and about a foot and a half in height. When he is thin, they become flaccid, and even hang down upon his sides.

He is never housed or otherwise sheltered, summer or winter.

He does not suffer more than other domestic animals from insects.

The only disease to which the Bactrian is known to be subject is a blistered tongue, which hinders him from eating, and he pines away. It is ascribed to bad fodder and lying on damp and dirty ground. The only remedy is cauterizing the blisters with a red-hot iron.

Horses, cattle, and sheep, though at first much afraid of the camel, soon become accustomed to him.

The average price of a pair of Bactrians is 175 silver rubles, but particularly fine animals sometimes sell as high as 300 silver rubles the pair.

The Bactrian is bred chiefly in the southernmost provinces of Russia. He does not multiply readily, more northwardly, although extensively used there.

Upon the whole, the use of the camel is rather declining in all the provinces most advanced in civilization.

# APPENDIX D.

### IMPORTATION OF CAMELS BY THE GOVERNMENT OF THE UNITED STATES.

HAVING been kindly permitted by the Hon. Jefferson Davis, Secretary of War, to examine the official correspondence between the War Department and the officers charged with the importation of the camel into the United States, I am enabled to furnish the following information on that interesting subject.

At the second session of the thirty-third Congress, the sum of thirty thousand dollars was appropriated for "importing camels for army transportation, and for other military purposes," with a view of testing their adaptation to our soil and climate, and to the service of the government as beasts of burden and transport. Major Henry C. Wayne, of the United States Army, was assigned to the duty of selection, purchase, and importation of the animals, and Lieut. D. D. Porter, of the Navy, was associated with him in the commission. The valuable services of Mr. Harris Heap, whose familiar acquaintance with the languages and customs of the countries where the camels were to be obtained, enabled him to be of great use to the officers detailed to this duty, were secured, and the storeship Supply, under command of Lieut. Porter, was ordered to proceed to the Levant to take the camels on board, and land them in Texas, where the climate and other circumstances were thought most favorable for commencing the experiment.

Upon his outward passage, Major Wayne visited London and Paris, and at the former city collected some particulars respecting the ability of the animal to bear a considerable change of climate and a long confinement, which are not without interest. Prof. Owen, perhaps the highest authority in England on such subjects, manifested much interest in Major Wayne's mission, and expressed the most entire confidence in the practicability of naturalizing the camel in the United States. At the Zoological Gardens, Major Wayne found two good specimens of the Egyptian burden camel. They had been five years at the Gardens, had never been affected with disease, and had bred two foals. Five camels have been born at the Gardens, three of which were reared. One imported camel lived twenty years in the menagerie of the Zoological Society, and was then sent to Ghent, where he lived at least three years longer. In winter, water is often frozen solid in their stalls at London, but they have not appeared to suffer from the cold. In summer, they consume fifteen pounds each, of coarse and inferior hay, and occasionally a little of the straw furnished for their litter. In winter, two quarts of oats, barley, or bran, per day, are added to their ration. The attendants thought them hardier than the coach horse, and, as before stated, they have never been affected by any troublesome malady. They are housed in winter, and no difficulty has been experienced in managing and controlling them.

Major Wayne found at Paris none of the French officers who had used the camel in Algeria, but procured a pamphlet by Gen. Daumas on the acclimatization of the camel in France. The pamphlet conveys little new information. It gives a list of the Arabic names of the plants on which the camel feeds, but many of these have not been identified by their European or scientific names. The list embraces one hundred and twenty species, certainly a pretty large proportion of the wild plants of Algeria. Besides vegetables commonly known as the food of the camel, I observe species of hyoscyamus and of terebinth, but I do not find the coloquintida, by either its officinal or its Arabic name, (hamdal,) nor any of the cactaceæ. Gen. Daumas describes a much more careful treatment of both dam and foal than is usual among the Bedouins, and observes that fodder on which blood has been spilt is believed to be poisonous to the camel.

Lieut. Porter visited Pisa, and saw the herd upon the Grand-ducal farm. He thinks they have not degenerated since their importation from Egypt, but on the contrary improved, and says that though neglected, overworked, never fed, but left to sustain themselves by browsing on the pine barrens, and not housed in winter, they are able to carry burdens of twelve hundred English pounds. With respect to their load, Lieut. Porter's information is much the same as was given me by the keepers, but I must observe that in December, 1849, I saw one hundred and forty of these animals stabled and regularly fed with hay at the Grand Duke's *cascine* near Pisa.

Major Wayne having joined the Supply, she proceeded to Tunis, where three camels were taken on board, with a view to test the arrangements which had been made by Lieut. Porter for their conveyance, and to experiment upon their management at sea, and the vessel proceeded to Constantinople, touching at Malta, Smyrna, and Salonica. The Supply arrived at Constantinople after a voyage of nearly ninety days from Tunis, and the camels did not appear to have suffered from either the long confinement on shipboard, or the rolling of the vessel in the heavy weather to which she was exposed. They consumed from eight to twelve pounds of hay and six quarts of oats per day each, and were watered once in three days, taking upon an average from two and a half to three buckets of water at a draught.

From Constantinople, Major Wayne and Lieut. Porter proceeded to Balaclava, where they saw both the Bactrian and the Arabian species. The inconvenience of accommodating a pack-saddle to the back of the two-humped camel was considered by the British officers a serious objection to the employment of that species for burden. It is not so tall as the Arabian, and slower of pace, but stronger. Col. McMurdo of the British Army, who had had great experience in the use of the Arabian camel in India, had a very high opinion of its value in the military service. Their burden, when employed by the British Army, he stated to average, under favorable circumstances, six hundred pounds, and their ordinary day's journey under this burden, "without pushing," from twenty-five to thirty miles. Gen. Napier organized in India a corps of five hundred camels, each carrying two men riding back to back, the forward rider being the groom and driver, the other a soldier. In action, the camels were formed into one or more squares, made to kneel, and hoppled. The soldiers were armed with rifles and sabres, and fought on foot. The corps would march seventy miles in twelve hours, and in the war in Sinde rendered efficient service. Gen. Simpson, of the British Army, informed Major Wayne that, when serving in India, he had five or six camels for his personal use, and preferred them to the best English horses, as being capable of longer marches. The only objection to their use was the difficulty of accustoming horses to them.

From Constantinople, the Supply proceeded to Alexandria, where some valuable animals were procured, one male from Sennaar, two from Siout, and one from the vicinity of Mount Sinai, a female from Muscat, and four from Siout, making nine in all, some of them for burden and some for the saddle. From Alexandria, Lieut. Porter writes, that one of the Tunisian camels, (two having been left at Constantinople,) had been on board one hundred and twenty days, and had improved in condition, upon an allowance of eight pounds of hay only per day.

They now sailed for Smyrna, and there purchased two male Bactrians, one cross between the male Bactrian and the female Arabian, four male, and fifteen female Arabians, one of which soon after produced a male foal. With this number, thirty-three in all, they sailed for the United States, and after putting into Kingston for water, they arrived on the coast of Texas early in May, with the loss, it is said, of but a single animal. Three Arabs and two Turks have accompanied them to the United States as grooms and drivers, and the entire cost of purchase and all contingent expenses has not exceeded eight thousand dollars.

This remarkable success in transporting so large animals to so great a distance on shipboard, furnishes a gratifying proof of the very judicious nature of the arrangements made by the officers for the performance of this difficult duty, and at the same time shows a power of endurance in the animal quite unexpected, thus fully justifying Major Wayne's opinion, that "the camel bears transportation by sea better than the horse, the mule, or the ox."

The officers have acted wisely in selecting varieties best adapted for general service. To have expended the funds at their command in obtaining animals of the swiftest breeds would have hazarded the success of the whole enterprise, while there can be little doubt, that in procuring camels from climates nearly corresponding with those in which they are to be naturalized, they have greatly increased the chances of a favorable result. With the Arabian and the Bactrian, we have the means of trying an *experimentum crucis*, on the adaptation of the hardier and more serviceable kinds to our conditions and wants, and with the experience which will be acquired from these, it will be comparatively an easy task to introduce, hereafter, breeds possessing any special qualities, which the more ordinary animal may be found to want.

It need hardly be added, that the opinions of Major Wayne and Lieut. Porter are entirely favorable to the success of the attempt to introduce and naturalize the camel, and that hitherto no unexpected obstacle or difficulty of any sort has presented itself.

The reader cannot but be struck with surprise at the extremely small quantity of nutriment consumed by the animals while on board the vessel. The opinion I had formed on this subject from personal observation, and expressed in Chapter IX. has been very fully confirmed. Doubtless in colder weather, and especially when exposed to severe labor, the camel will require a more liberal supply of food, but even under the most unfavorable circumstances, there is no probability that the cost of his keeping will approach that of the horse. Indeed, upon most routes where he will be employed, he will require no nutriment but those plants with which nature has sown the desert, as if for his especial sustenance. I find no satisfactory evidence that he feeds on any of the cacti, but though he may reject these plants at first, it is not improbable that he may learn to eat them, as thirst has taught the mule in South America to feed upon the melon-cactus or rather to drink its juices, in spite of the formidable spines with which it is armed.[1] The foliage and especially

[1] Humboldt, *Ansichten der Natur*, I. *Steppen und Wüsten.* Cattle are fed upon cacti in New Mexico, the spines being burnt off.

the seed-pods and seeds of the mezquit would doubtless prove a very acceptable and nutritious diet to the camel. The mezquit appears closely to resemble the *sont* or gum arabic tree of the Arabian and Libyan deserts. I have often tempted the camel with the seed-vessels of this acacia, and found, that he would turn from beans, otherwise a favorite food, to devour them. The mezquit yields a large crop of seeds, and these do not fall with the leaf, but the pod remains attached to the branches, still unopened until after the appearance of the new leaf. There is consequently no period of the year, when it does not furnish either foliage or seeds, and as it is found almost everywhere upon the plains, there is reason to believe that independently of other vegetables indigenous to the American desert, the mezquit alone would provide abundantly for the support of the camel, over very wide tracts which yield little or no food for the horse or the ox.

# INDEX.

# INDEX.